Helen Pridham is a freelance journalist who has specialized in personal finance for over twenty years. She has written for *The Times*, the *Sunday Times*, *Money Observer*, *Investors Chronicle*, the *Herald* in Glasgow and other publications. She has won a number of awards and commendations for financial journalism. Her previously published books include *Making the Most of Your Money* and *Tax and Finance for Women*.

G000108722

THE SUNDAY TIMES
Personal Finance Guide to

YOUR PENSION

How to Invest for Future Security

Helen Pridham

HarperCollins*Publishers*

HarperCollins*Publishers*
77–85 Fulham Palace Road,
Hammersmith, London W6 8JB

A Paperback Original 1998
1 3 5 7 9 8 6 4 2

First published in Great Britain by
HaperCollins*Publishers* 1996

ISBN 0 00 653049 4

Set in Times by
Rowland Phototypesetting Ltd,
Bury St Edmunds, Suffolk

Printed and bound in Great Britain by
Caledonian International Book Manufacturing Ltd, Glasgow

CONTENTS

ACKNOWLEDGEMENTS

I would like to thank the many people who assisted me with this book. In particular my thanks go to Nigel Webb of Equitable Life, Lyn Webb of Legal & General and Andy Agar of Norwich Union for their help and expert advice. I would also like to express my gratitude to Roger Key of Watson Wyatt, Peter Quinton of the Annuity Bureau and John Turton of Best Investment.

INTRODUCTION

The first state pension for elderly people on low incomes was introduced in Britain at the beginning of the 20th century. Pensions have come a long way since then, but many retired people today still suffer financial hardship. Don't let this happen to you. If you want to ensure you have an adequate retirement income, you must take action now to improve your pension.

The current Government has made reform of pensions one of its main priorities. It is keen to see retirement incomes improve – but not at the state's expense. It wants everyone to have their own private pension and is proposing the introduction of stakeholder pensions for this purpose.

One of the reasons why many people fail to make proper retirement provision is that they find pensions too confusing. This book is designed to guide you through the maze and equip you with the information you need to make the right decisions about your future pension plans.

The Story So Far – a Potted History of State Pensions

1908   A means-tested flat-rate non-contributory pension (the Lloyd George Pension) introduced for 70-year-olds

1925   Contributory retirement pensions brought in, payable at 65; widows' pensions introduced for those on lower incomes

1943   Discretionary national system of means-tested benefits introduced for elderly people

1948   'Beveridge' system of universal contributory pensions launched for men at 65 and women at 60

1961   Graduated retirement pension introduced (abolished in 1975)

1978   State Earnings Related Pension Scheme (SERPS) introduced for employees to provide an additional income-related benefit on top of the basic retirement pension

1986   Plans announced to reduce SERPS pensions to be phased in between 2000 and 2010

1988   Employees given the choice of opting out of SERPS and having National Insurance rebates paid into an appropriate personal pension instead

1993   Announcement of equal retirement age of 65 for men and women to be phased in between 2010 and 2020

1998   Plans for stakeholder pensions announced . . .

Why You Need a Pension

Being able to look forward to a good pension means being able to look forward to an enjoyable retirement. With a good pension, you can do all the things you do not have time for while you are working – travel more, play more golf – without worrying about how you are going to pay the bills. Without an adequate retirement income, your life could turn to a miserable hand-to-mouth existence.

To be sure of having enough pension you will need to take matters into your own hands. The state can no longer afford to provide an adequate pension for everyone. The basic state pension has been shrinking steadily in value since 1979 and a single person's pension is now worth just 17% of average earnings.

If you are fortunate, you may have a pension with your job so your employer will be contributing to a pension on your behalf. But you still need to check whether this scheme will provide you with enough retirement income, especially if your service with your employer is limited. You will often need to top up your contributions. If you don't belong to a company pension scheme, you must make sure you pay enough into a personal plan to build up your own retirement savings.

Few people stay in the same employment throughout their working life. Most switch between jobs and go in and out of company pension schemes or have employment breaks. This can lead to their pension arrangements becoming rather complicated.

Although pensions can appear complex in essence they are simply a tax-efficient form of saving for retirement. It is the 'wrappers' they come in that often create confusion. One of the main aims of this book is to demystify the subject: the more you know about your pension the easier it is to plan your retirement successfully and make the best use of the opportunities available.

Before going into detail about the various types of pension and what happens to your pension in different situations such as breaks in employment or divorce, this chapter deals with basic considerations such as why pensions are such a good way of saving for retirement, suggests an action plan for different age groups, and explains how to assess any pensions you may already have.

Retirement – It's Longer than You Think

One of the reasons why it is now more important than ever before to plan properly for retirement is that people are stopping work earlier and earlier and living longer and longer. Retirement used to be regarded as a relatively brief part of a person's life. Once you stopped working you were seen as having 'one foot in the grave'. Nowadays nothing could be further from the truth. People reaching retirement age are fitter and healthier than ever before and are looking forward to enjoying an active 'third age'.

Yet many people are still unaware just how long their retirement might last and as a result tend to underestimate the amount they need to save to see them comfortably through that period. They do not realize that if they delay too long the time they spend drawing a pension could be longer than the time they spent saving for it.

You must plan for the long term – around 20 years or even longer. As Table 1 shows, at the present state retirement age – 65 for men and 60 for women – both sexes can expect on average to live to over 80. Those are individual life expectancies. If you are living with a partner, one of you can expect to live to over 89!

Table 1: How long will you need a pension?

Male/Female Age	Male	Female	One of a couple (male and female same age)
55	26	31	35
60	22	27	30
65	18	22	26
70	14	18	21
75	12	14	17

Average life expectancy in years

Source: Equitable Life

Naturally, some people will die earlier than the average but there will also be those who live longer. Around half of those individuals who reach retirement age will live longer than the number of years shown in the table.

To put these periods in perspective, think back to what you were doing twenty years ago and all that has happened since – how your income has risen, how prices have increased, how much money you have spent. The need to build up a realistic amount of pension provision will then become even clearer. Providing a comfortable amount of retirement income over periods like these does not come cheap! If you would like to retire early, you will have to plan for an even longer period. It is an option that many people are choosing nowadays or being forced to choose owing to redundancy. Recent figures show that around half of all men and women within five years of the state retirement age are no longer working. Early retirement, however, means there will be fewer years in which you can contribute to a pension and therefore less time for your savings to grow. So you will need to be even more careful about whether you are saving enough.

Why a Pension?

A pension is not the only way of saving for retirement, but it is one of the most tax-efficient. Governments have provided a number of tax incentives to encourage people to save for their retirement in a disciplined, long-term way.

There are three main tax advantages of pensions:

- **Tax relief on contributions.** Your savings qualify for income tax relief. This means that Government pays back the income tax it would otherwise taken from the money you invest in a pension. So for every £77 a basic rate taxpayer contributes to a pension, the tax man adds another £23 bringing the total investment of £100, giving a pension an automatic headstart on any other form of saving. Although there are limits on how much you can contribute, relatively few people save enough for these to be a problem.
- **Favourable tax treatment of pension funds.** Although the funds in which you invest your pension contributions are not treated quite as favourably now as they were in the past – before July 1997 they could reclaim tax on UK share dividends – they have other tax benefits. They do not pay tax on other forms of investment income and any capital gains they make are also tax free.
- **Tax free cash at retirement.** You don't have to take all your pension as a regular income; part of your fund can be taken as a tax-free lump sum. The amount depends on the type of scheme. In the case of personal pensions, for example, up to 25% of your fund can be taken as a lump sum. This money can be used to pay off any outstanding debts when you reach retirement, make a major purchase such as a new car or treat yourself to a 'once-in-a-lifetime' holiday.

Don't Delay

Once you have recognized the importance of pensions, it is vital to act as quickly as possible to start or increase your contributions. This may be difficult when there are many other demands on your money. But any amount you can set aside now is better than nothing because, when it comes to pensions, time is quite literally money. Waiting means not only that you may save less, but there is less time for your savings to grow.

You may still feel that waiting a year or two won't matter very much. However, the figures in Table 2 show that the cost of delaying just one year can be significant and that the younger you are when you delay, the greater the impact.

Table 2: The cost of delay

Projected pension funds based on gross savings of £50 a month

Starting age	Pension fund at 60	Contributions saved	Loss of fund
24	£110,000		
25	£101,000	£600	£9,000
34	£44,800		
35	£40,700	£600	£4,100
44	£16,500		
45	£14,700	£600	£1,800

Source: Norwich Union, based on growth rate of 9% p.a.

What You Should be Doing

Whatever age you are, there is nearly always something you can do to improve your pension prospects. Below are some key areas which different age groups need to consider; several are the same whatever your age group – for more detailed information, see the relevant chapters.

Pension priorities for Twentysomethings

- If an employer offers you membership of a pension scheme it is usually a good idea to accept. If you don't, you are effectively agreeing to a pay cut, because you will be missing out on the contributions your employer would be making to the scheme on your behalf.
- Start your own personal pension plan if you can't become a

member of a company pension scheme, but make sure it can be adapted – at no extra cost – to changes in your future circumstances.

- If you are an employee and are currently paying into the State Earnings Related Pension Scheme (SERPS), consider opting out and having part of your National Insurance contributions paid into an appropriate personal pension. But you must pay extra voluntary contributions (AVCs) to be sure of a decent pension.

- If you have no pension and are planning to buy your first home, consider taking out a pension mortgage if money is short. That way you will be killing two birds with one stone. But resolve to separate your mortgage and pension as soon as you can afford it, otherwise you will have to sacrifice the cash sum from your pension at retirement to repay the loan.

Pension priorities for Thirtysomethings

- If an employer offers you membership of a pension scheme it is usually a good idea to accept. If you don't, you are effectively agreeing to a pay cut, because you will be missing out on the contributions your employer would be making to the scheme on your behalf.

- If you have turned down pension scheme membership in the past, ask your employer if you can change your mind.

- Consider topping up your pension with additional voluntary contributions (AVCs), especially if you think you might like to retire early.

- Start your own personal pension plan if you can't become a member of a company pension scheme, but make sure it can be adapted – at no extra cost – to changes in your future circumstances.

- If you are an employee, ask your employer to contribute to your personal pension. If you have no luck, consider making a 'salary sacrifice' next time you get a pay rise and have your employer pay this directly into your pension. No National Insurance must be paid on this money, so more can be paid in than if you received it first.

- If you already have a personal pension plan, try to increase your contributions on a regular basis. But before topping up your existing plan check whether you could get better terms elsewhere.
- If you are an employee and are currently paying into the State Earnings Related Pension Scheme (SERPS), consider opting out and having part of your National Insurance contributions paid into an appropriate personal pension. But you must pay extra voluntary contributions to be sure of a decent pension.

Pension priorities for Fortysomethings

- If an employer offers you membership of a pension scheme it is usually a good idea to accept. If you don't, you are effectively agreeing to a pay cut, because you will be missing out on the contributions your employer would be making to the scheme on your behalf.
- If you have turned down pension scheme membership in the past, ask your employer if you can change your mind.
- Even if you have been a member of an employer's scheme for a while, consider topping up your pension with additional voluntary contributions (AVCs). But if you are already making AVCs and you have been a member of the same pension scheme all or most of your working life, check you are not overfunding.
- Start your own personal pension plan if you can't become a member of a company pension scheme, but make sure it can be adapted – at no extra cost – to changes in your future circumstances.
- If you are an employee, ask your employer to contribute to your personal pension. If you have no luck, consider making a 'salary sacrifice' next time you get a pay rise and have your employer pay this directly into your pension. No National Insurance must be paid on this money, so more can be paid in than if you received it first.

- If you already have a personal pension plan, try to increase your contributions on a regular basis. Extra lump sums can also be invested in one-off single premium pension plans. Before topping up your existing plan check whether you could get better terms elsewhere.

- If you have failed to make maximum contributions to a personal pension in the past, you could top up your savings going back up to six years by investing a lump sum. Tax relief will be payable.

- Women in their mid-forties who are contracted out of the State Earnings Related Pension Scheme (SERPS) into an appropriate personal pension should seek the advice of their pension company or financial adviser to check whether they would be better off contracting back into SERPS.

Pension priorities for Fiftysomethings

- If an employer offers you membership of a pension scheme it is usually a good idea to accept. If you don't, you are effectively agreeing to a pay cut, because you will be missing out on the contributions your employer would be making to the scheme on your behalf.

- If you have turned down pension scheme membership in the past, ask your employer if you can change your mind.

- Even if you have been a member of an employer's scheme for a while, consider topping up your pension with additional voluntary contributions (AVCs). But if you are already making AVCs and you have been a member of the same pension scheme all or most of your working life check you are not overfunding.

- Start your own personal pension plan if you cannot become a member of a company pension scheme, but make sure you will not be penalized if you take early retirement.

- If you are an employee, ask your employer to contribute to your personal pension. If you have no luck, consider making a 'salary sacrifice' next time you get a pay rise and have your employer pay this directly into your pension. No National

Insurance must be paid on this money, so more can be paid in than if you received it first.

- If you already have a personal pension plan, try to increase your contributions on a regular basis. Extra lump sums can also be invested in one-off single premium pension plans. But before topping up your existing plan check whether you could get better terms elsewhere.
- If you have failed to make maximum contributions to a personal pension in the past, you could top up your savings going back up to six years by investing a lump sum. Tax relief will be payable.
- Consider the investment strategy of your personal pension as you approach retirement. It may be sensible to move your money gradually from a share invested fund to one which invests in fixed interest securities to protect your fund against a sharp fall in the stock market just as you get to retirement.
- If you are contracted out of the State Earnings Related Pension Scheme (SERPS) into an appropriate personal pension you should seek the advice of your pension company or financial adviser to check whether you would be better off contracting back into SERPS.

How Much Pension Have You Already Got?

Before you decide exactly what to do next, you should work out what, if any, pension entitlement you already have. This may require some detective work if you have changed jobs a few times in the past.

If you have worked for the same employer and been a member of that employer's pension scheme all your life, it will not be too difficult. The same would be true if you have never been a member of a company pension scheme but have contributed regularly to a retirement annuity or personal pension instead. In both cases, you should be receiving regular annual statements showing how much your pension might be worth when you retire.

However, over 90% of the population do not fit neatly into either of these categories. Most people move between several different employers during their working life, some with and some without pension schemes. If you have been a member of an employer's pension scheme in the past, you may have left pension benefits behind or been given a refund of contributions. You may have started a personal pension and then stopped your contributions.

To add to the complexity, company pension regulations have changed several times in recent years which will also affect your rights. Nowadays you only have to complete two years' service as a member of an employer's scheme before becoming entitled to pension benefits, but before 6 April 1988 you usually had to complete five years' pensionable service. Until January 1986 there was no obligation for employers' pension schemes to provide 'transfer values' of employees' pension benefits when they left. Today you have a right to a transfer value.

This means that you may have a number of 'dormant' pensions waiting in old schemes for you to reach retirement, and they may be pensions of different types. Some may have been based on your salary at the time you left your old employer and others may be 'money purchase' schemes where you had a 'pot' of money built up from your own and your employer's contributions.

When you left your old employer a statement of benefits will have been given to you. What those benefits are now worth and will be worth by the time you retire will depend on the type of scheme and when you left:

- **The current value of a pension left in a salary-based pension scheme:** Generally speaking, if you left a salary-based pension scheme on or after 1 January 1986, your pension will have been revalued in line with inflation ever since and will continue to be so until you retire. So its purchasing power when you retire should be the same as it is now. If you left before 1 January 1986, the same may apply but the situation differs from scheme to scheme. In some cases, your pension may have remained the same in money terms as it was when you left. So it will be worth a lot less now because of inflation and this erosion will continue until you eventually reach retirement.

- **The current value of a pension left in a 'money purchase' company scheme or personal pension.** If your old scheme was a money purchase scheme, your 'pot' of money would have remained invested and would have continued to enjoy any investment growth achieved by the managers of the scheme. The same would be true if you had ceased contributions to a retirement annuity or personal pension in the past, although some pension companies' on-going charges on individual paid-up policies of this kind can be vicious.

To find out about pensions left in old employers' schemes, you should write to the trustees and ask. If you have lost touch and don't know where to write, contact the Registrar of Pension Schemes in Newcastle (0191 225 6394) which operates a free tracing service. In the case of retirement annuity or personal pension policies, providers should be sending you regular statements, unless you have moved house and forgotten to tell them.

However, even when you know the present value of the pension 'pot' you have in an old money purchase company scheme or personal pension, you will still have some further work to do to establish what it may be worth to you in pension terms when you get to retirement. An exact calculation is impossible, as the end result will depend on future investment growth, inflation and annuity rates when you retire, none of which can be predicted precisely. The following tables can help to give you a rough idea, though. Table 3 shows how much each £10,000 of your pension may be worth in the future at different growth rates. Table 4 shows very roughly how much pension you will get at different annuity rates. (These will depend largely on long-term interest rates when your retire.) However, purchasing an annuity which provides a growing income will be considerably more expensive. Table 5 shows how inflation reduces the value of your money.

Table 3: How money grows

How much £10,000 will increase at different growth rates over different time periods.

Years	Growth rate				
	4%	6%	8%	10%	12%
5	12,170	13,380	14,690	16,110	17,620
10	14,800	17,910	21,590	25,940	31,060
15	18,010	23,970	31,720	41,770	54,740
20	21,910	32,070	46,610	67,270	96,460
25	26,660	42,920	68,480	108,350	170,000
30	32,430	57,430	100,630	174,490	299,600

Table 4: How much pension you can buy

A rough guide to how much pension you can expect from a lump sum at different annuity rates.

Pension fund	Annuity rate		
	5%	7.5%	10%
	£p.a.	£p.a.	£p.a.
£10,000	£500	£750	£1,000
£25,000	£1,250	£1,875	£2,500
£50,000	£2,500	£3,750	£5,000
£100,000	£5,000	£7,500	£10,000
£200,000	£10,000	£15,000	£20,000

Table 5: The effect of inflation

How much £1,000 in today's money is worth at the end of different periods at various rates of inflation.

Years	Inflation rate				
	2%	3%	4%	5%	6%
5	906	863	822	784	747
10	820	744	676	614	558
15	743	642	555	481	417
20	673	554	456	377	312
25	610	478	375	295	233
30	552	412	308	231	174

How Much You Should Be Saving for the Future

When you have found out what, if any, pension you already have under your belt, you can start to work out how much you should be saving for the future. The answer will depend on how much income you want to have in retirement.

Most people are prepared to see their income go down when they stop working because they expect their expenditure to fall, too. Their mortgage will usually be paid off and work-related costs, such as travel, will also disappear. Still, to maintain the same standard of living it is generally agreed that you need a pension equal to at least 50%, if not 70%, of your pre-retirement income.

The later you start to save, the more you will need to set aside to achieve such a goal. According to the Association of British Insurers (ABI), in order to have a pension of one-half of annual pay from age 65, the amount that must be contributed annually to a pension is 20% of your earnings if contributions start at age 30, 35% if contributions start at age 40 and as much as 80% if contributions start at age 50!

Table 6: Your potential pension fund

How much your pension fund may be worth at retirement at different levels of monthly savings assuming a growth rate of 6%.

	Pension fund assuming 6% p.a. growth					
Your retirement age		*Age 60*			*Age 65*	
Your age now	30	40	50	30	40	50
	£	£	£	£	£	£
Your gross monthly savings						
£50	48,977	22,783	8,165	69,034	33,980	14,415
£100	97,953	45,565	16,330	138,067	67,960	28,830
£200	195,906	91,130	32,660	276,136	135,920	57,660

How to get the best out of your pension and make extra savings within different types of pension schemes are discussed in the following chapters.

The goal of most people will simply be to build up as much extra pension as possible from the savings they can afford. Table 6 indicates the funds you could build up saving different amounts over different periods – but don't forget that the growth rate of 6% is completely hypothetical and no allowance is made for inflation. If your savings grow faster the funds will be bigger but if growth is lower they will be less and inflation will reduce their real value in any case. So no one can afford to be complacent.

Stakeholder Pensions

In order to encourage every one to save towards a second pension on top of the state scheme, the Government is intending to introduce stakeholder pensions.

The aim is to make these pensions simple, secure, flexible and low cost. They will be particularly useful for the low paid and those who have not been well-served by existing pension arrangements. However, it is probably not a good idea for anyone currently considering joining a pension scheme or setting up their own pension to wait until stakeholder pensions are launched. As shown in Table 2 above, delaying your pension even by just a year can cost you dear.

1 ‖ *State Pensions*

Most people can expect to get some pension from the state when they reach official retirement age. Men qualify for this pension at 65. Women are currently eligible at 60, but in the year 2020 the state pension age is to be equalized at 65. The changeover won't take place overnight, however. It will be phased in over ten years.

As Table 7 shows, this means that women born between April 1950 and April 1955 will have a state pension age somewhere between 60 and 65, but for women born after April 1955 the age will be 65. (See Booklet NP 46, available from Social Security offices, for the full table of retirement ages during the transition period.)

Table 7: How the equalization of state pension ages will affect women born between April 1950 and April 1955

Date of birth	Pensionable age	Pension date
06/04/50 to 05/05/50	60yrs–60yrs 1 mth	06/05/2010
06/10/50 to 05/11/50	60yrs 6mths–60yrs 7mths	06/05/2011
06/04/51 to 05/05/51	61yrs–61yrs 1mth	06/05/2012
06/10/51 to 05/11/51	61yrs 6mths–61yrs 7mths	06/05/2013
06/04/52 to 05/05/52	62yrs–62yrs 1mth	06/05/2014
06/10/52 to 05/11/52	62yrs 6mths–62yrs 7mths	06/05/2015
06/04/53 to 05/05/53	63yrs–63yrs 1mth	06/05/2016
06/10/53 to 05/11/53	63yrs 6mths–63yrs 7mths	06/05/2017
06/04/54 to 05/05/54	64yrs–64yrs 1mth	06/05/2018
06/10/54 to 05/11/54	64yrs 6mths–64yrs 7mths	06/05/2019
06/04/55	65yrs	06/04/2020

Source: DSS booklet NP46, 'A Guide to Retirement Pensions'

The amount of state pension you get will vary. It depends on such factors as your National Insurance contribution record, when you started work and possibly your marital status. Your pension could consist of up to three different elements: the basic retirement pension, graduated retirement benefit and an addition from the state earnings related pension scheme (SERPS). Doing the sums yourself to find out what state pension you will get is not easy.

Table 8: State pension rates for the 1998/99 tax year

	Per Week	Per Year
Single person's pension	£64.70	£3,364.40
Widow's pension (from age 55)	£64.70	£3.364.40
Married woman's pension	£38.70	£2,012.40
Married couple's pension	£103.40	£5,376.80
Maximum graduated		
pension: Man	£7.22	£375.44
Woman	£6.05	£314.60

If you want to find out the total pension you can expect from the state, the simplest thing is to ask for a 'pension forecast' from the Department of Social Security. You will need to complete form BR19 which can be obtained from your local DSS office. If your circumstances are straightforward you should get your forecast in about three to six weeks, but it may take a little longer if you are widowed or divorced.

A state pension is not paid automatically. You must claim it. However, you will normally be sent a claim form (BR1) when you are within about four months of state pension age. Men will normally receive two claim forms so that if they are married their wives can also claim. If you do not receive a form, contact your local DSS. When you receive the form you will also be sent details of the pensions for which you qualify. You will be able to choose between having the pension paid directly into your bank account or by a book of orders which you cash in at the post office.

The Basic State Retirement Pension

Contrary to what many people believe, the basic state retirement pension is not a universal right. You must have paid or been credited with a certain number of years of National Insurance contributions to qualify. Someone who has made insufficient contributions may receive a reduced pension, but you will normally need to have made at least ten years' contributions to qualify for any pension at all.

Another frequent misapprehension about state pensions is that they are tax free. They are not. However, if the basic pension is your only or main income, it will fall within your personal allowance so no tax will be payable.

Who qualifies?

As a general rule you must have paid full rate National Insurance contributions for 90% of your working life to qualify for a full pension. Only full years of contributions count and these are known as 'qualifying' years. A year for this purpose corresponds to the tax year, which runs from 6 April to the following 5 April.

The DSS considers your working life to start from the beginning of the tax year in which you reach age 16 and finish at the end of the tax year before the one in which you reach state pension age. So to clock up the required record, men must have contributed for at least 44 qualifying years and women for 39. By the year 2020, women will also need to have contributed for 44 years.

If your contribution record is less than the amount required for a full pension, you may get a reduced benefit. However you must normally have at least 10 qualifying years to be eligible for the minimum basic pension of 25% of the full rate.

Table 9: How much basic pension will you qualify for?

Men		Women	
No. of qualifying years	% of pension	No. of qualifying years	% of pension
0–10	Nil	0–9	Nil
11	25%	10	26%
15	35%	15	39%
20	46%	20	52%
25	57%	25	65%
30	69%	30	77%
35	80%	35	90%
40	91%	39+	100%
44+	100%		

Source: DSS booklet NP46, 'A Guide to Retirement Pensions'

Not all gaps in your record will harm your pension prospects. Children who remain at school until age 18 are credited with contributions (although students in higher education are not). If you are unemployed or off work due to incapacity, credits will also be provided as long as you receive Jobseekers Allowance, are registering as unemployed or receive sickness benefit. Men aged 60 or over who have stopped working will also receive NI credits automatically up to age 65.

Home Responsibilities Protection

Fewer years of contributions are required to qualify for a full basic pension if you have received Home Responsibilities Protection (HRP). HRP has been available for complete tax years since April 1978 to help protect the basic pension of people who take time off work to care for children or look after someone who is sick or disabled. HRP is given automatically if you are receiving child benefit for a child under age 16, or are getting income support so that you can look after a sick or disabled person at home.

If you are not getting these benefits you may still qualify. If, for example, you are regularly looking after someone for at least 35 hours a week who is getting attendance allowance or a similar benefit. In these circumstances, you will need to apply for HRP on form CF411 'How to protect your state retirement pension if you are looking after someone at home' available from your local DSS office. When your basic pension is worked out, the number of years for which you get HRP is taken away from the number of qualifying years needed to calculate your pension. For a full basic pension, however, HRP cannot reduce the number of qualifying years below 20.

At present HRP covers basic pension only. Arrangements are being made to extend HRP coverage to the state earnings related pension scheme for those retiring (or widowed) on or after 6 April 1999.

Part time workers

Even if you have been working, you may not necessarily have been building up qualifying years for a state pension if you were on low earnings. Anyone paid less than the 'lower earnings limit' (£3,328 for 1998/99) does not have to make NI contributions. You may, though, still qualify for HRP or you could consider making Class 3 voluntary contributions to ensure your NI record is adequate to qualify for a pension (see below). For more information get DSS form CA08 'National Insurance voluntary contributions'.

Married women

Only around 28% of retired women currently receive a full basic pension based on their own contribution record. This is mainly because in the past married women could opt to pay a reduced rate of NI contribution, often known as the 'married woman's stamp'. The option has not been available since April 1977 to newly married women, or women going back to work after two years out of employment, but some continue to pay these reduced rate contributions.

The snag with these contributions is that they conferred no pension entitlement. A married woman was able to claim under her husband's NI record, but this only entitles her to a spouse's pension which is worth 40% less than the ordinary single person's pension. The husband's single person's pension plus the spouse's pension are what is normally referred to as the married couple's pension.

However, a married woman cannot receive the spouse's pension until her husband has reached state pension age and claimed his own pension. If she reaches 60 first and qualifies for a reduced amount of state pension in her own right, she can take that pension initially and then have it topped up to the amount of the spouse's pension when her husband retires.

Boosting Your Basic State Pension

- **Voluntary NI contributions.** To ensure you receive a full basic pension, or a larger proportion than you are at present entitled to, you could consider paying Class 3 voluntary NI contributions. These can be used to fill up gaps of a few months or even years in your contribution record. Because only complete years of contributions count towards your pension, they may be particularly worthwhile if you have worked and paid full contributions for most of a year which would be excluded from the reckoning if you do not complete the year.

  A statement will normally be sent to you pointing out such a shortfall around 18 months after the end of the tax year. It will tell you how many Class 3 contributions you need to pay to make up the difference. You have up to six years to make up for missing contributions with voluntary ones. But they may not always be a good idea. For example, unless you are likely to end up with at least 10 qualifying years, you won't be eligible for a pension anyway. If you are a married or divorced woman, you may get a better pension claiming on your husband's NI record. For further information on voluntary contributions see DSS leaflet CA07 'National Insurance – unpaid and late contributions', and CA08 'National Insurance voluntary contributions'.

- **Delaying your retirement.** You can increase your pension by deferring it. For every year you delay, it will be increased by 7.5% with pro rata increases for shorter periods. This increase will apply to each element of your pension – basic, graduated and SERPS. At present it is only possible to defer for a maximum of five years, but from 6 April 2010 it will be possible to put it off indefinitely. The annual increment to the value of the pension will also be increased to 10.4%. For further information see DSS leaflet NI92 'Giving up your Retirement Pension to earn extra'.

- **Claiming Income Support.** The basic state pension is less than the Income Support level. So if you have no other income you can claim Income Support to top up your income. You may also be eligible for other means tested benefits. Many retired people fail to claim all the benefits to which they are entitled.

Graduated Retirement Benefit

If you were employed between April 1961 and April 1975 and earned more than around £9 a week you will have paid graduated NI contributions. These qualify you for a graduated pension benefit. The amount you get will depend on how many 'units' of graduated contributions you paid at the time and the value of the units when you claim your pension. For 1998/99 each unit is worth 8.4p. Once in payment the units are uprated each year in line with inflation.

The maximum number of units is 72 for a woman and 86 for a man. To work out the number of units you have, add together all your graduated contributions, divide the total by 9 for a woman, and 7.5 for a man, and round up any odd half-unit to the next whole number. From 6 April 2010 women in receipt of graduated retirement benefit will have their units calculated on the same basis as men.

State Earnings Related Pension Scheme (SERPS)

SERPS was introduced in April 1978 to provide all employees with an additional income-related pension. It relates to the band of earnings on which NI contributions are paid, between what are known as the lower and upper earnings limits. It was originally designed to provide a pension of 25% of the best of these earnings averaged over 20 years. The Conservative administration radically revised the scheme in 1988, bringing down the pension entitlement to 20% of earnings averaged over an employee's whole working life. This reduction is still being phased in between 1999 and 2009.

Who qualifies?

Originally every employee who paid NI insurance contributions was a member of SERPS, unless they were a member of an employer's pension scheme that had 'contracted out' of SERPS and was providing a replacement pension. Otherwise only the self-employed were excluded.

After 1988, it became possible for individual members to 'opt out' of the scheme and have part of their NI contributions rebated and paid into a personal pension plan on their behalf instead. To encourage people to opt out the Government paid an extra bonus into their personal pensions plans for the first five years after the scheme was introduced.

How much?

Unlike the basic state pension, which requires a minimum contribution period of around ten years before you qualify for any benefits at all, you start building up your SERPS benefits from day one. Your right to SERPS does not depend on your right to a basic pension.

How your SERPS pension is worked out partly depends on whether you retire before or after 6 April 2000 because of the phased-in reduction in SERPS benefits. Basically, if you retire before then you will get 25% of your total band earnings for each year since 1978/79, revalued in line with the rise in national average earnings, divided by the number of years you have worked since then. If you retire afterwards, the percentage applied to your earnings from 1988/89 will be reduced on a sliding scale from 25% to 20% depending on the year in which you reach pension age.

For more information on how your SERPS pension is calculated, see DSS leaflet NP46 'A guide to retirement pensions'. Alternatively, if you request a pension forecast, it will include a calculation of any SERPS pension you may be due.

Why you may not get a SERPS pension

Apart from the self-employed, who have not had to contribute to SERPS, employees may not be members of SERPS if they worked for an employer with a contracted-out pension scheme or made the decision to opt out of SERPS after 1988 into their own private pension.

Company Schemes

If you have spent time since 1978 as a member of a company pension scheme which is 'contracted out' of SERPS, you and your employer will have paid less National Insurance and you will receive a replacement pension from your employer's scheme for that period of your working life instead.

Until April 1997, the pension you received from a final salary-related company scheme had to be a guaranteed minimum of no less than the SERPS pension given up. Companies are no longer obliged to give such guarantees for pensions built up since that date, although the pension provided must fulfil certain criteria. For example, the build-up rate must be at least one-eightieth of final salary for each year of service. A 50% spouse's pension must be provided and the pension itself must increase in line with the retail price index up to a maximum of 5% p.a.

Company schemes run on a 'money purchase' basis – where the final pension is largely investment related rather than a defined amount of salary – have not normally had to provide a guaranteed minimum pension. Instead, the company must put into the scheme a sum of at least the difference between the full and reduced National Insurance contributions it pays as a result of being contracted out. The fund built up from these contributions is known as the 'protected rights' element and it must be used to buy an annuity which provides a pension that increases in line with the retail price index up to a maximum of 5% p.a.

and has a 50% spouse's pension. The starting amount of pension it provides will depend on such factors as annuity rates at the time of retirement. (For more details see next section on 'appropriate personal pensions', to which the same rules apply.)

Appropriate Personal Pensions

Since 1988, employees who were not members of 'contracted out' pension schemes have had the choice of opting out of SERPS and having their own personal pension schemes instead. They pay National Insurance contributions as usual, but the DSS rebates part of their own and their employers' contributions to their chosen personal pension provider after the end of each tax year. The policies into which the rebates are paid are known as 'appropriate personal pensions' and the fund which is built up from them is known as the 'protected rights' fund.

Clearly, it is only worth opting out of SERPS into a personal pension if you are likely to get a better pension at retirement. There was never any guarantee of this because the pension you get at retirement from this type of plan depends on a variety of factors, such as the level of charges deducted by the pension provider, the investment returns and the annuity rates available when you retire. However, the more money that is put into the plan the greater the likelihood that you will get a better pension, so the main factor influencing the decision to opt out has been the size of the National Insurance rebate provided.

When opting out of SERPS was first introduced, the decision as to whether it was worthwhile was fairly straightforward. Initially it was suggested that men below the age of about 50 and women below about 43 should consider opting out, provided they were earning more than around £10,000 a year and expected to remain contracted out of SERPS for at least five years. Since then, the National Insurance rebate has varied considerably and it has become a much less clear-cut decision. Anyone who has opted out in the past should certainly review their position to see if they would not be better off opting back into

SERPS. Even for younger people considering opting out for the first time, it has become a less attractive option.

Initially the rebate which was paid into your personal pension was a flat amount. For the first five years, from 6 April 1988, it was 5.8% of band earnings (the income on which you pay National Insurance contributions between the upper and lower earnings limits). To encourage people to opt out, the Government also provided an extra 2% bonus for the first five years on top of the basic rebate. This gave a total rebate of 7.8% and tax relief was also given on the employee's portion of the basic rebate.

After April 1993 there was a flat rebate of 4.8% of band earnings, with 1% extra for those aged 30 or over. In April 1997 age-related rebates were introduced, starting at 3.4% at age 15 and increasing to a maximum of 9%. For a man aged 30 on average earnings of £18,500, this produced a rebate worth £651 per year. However, following the Chancellor's decision to abolish tax relief on dividends received by pension funds in the July 1997 Budget, it was announced that rebates would be increased marginally from April 1999. They will rise from 3.4% to 3.8% for the youngest ages, with proportionately smaller increases at other ages, but the maximum is to remain 9%.

The consensus among pension providers is that men older than about 52 and women older than about 45 should now consider contracting back into SERPS. For younger employees the decision is less straightforward. Whether or not continuing to contract out will result in better benefits being received from a personal pension plan will depend on the extent to which future investment returns are better than increases in earnings.

The type of personal pension most likely to achieve better investment returns will be one invested fully in a fund of shares. However, these funds are risky; their values will go up and down so investors have to be prepared to accept this extra risk. To find out whether it would be worthwhile for you to opt out of SERPS or back into it again, you should seek the advice of your pension company or a financial adviser.

What you get

If you have opted out of SERPS in the past and had your rebates paid into an appropriate personal pension, the pension you get at retirement will depend on the size of the fund you build up – the protected rights fund – and the annuity rates available when you retire. The size of the fund will be determined by the charges deducted by the pension company and, more importantly, by the investment returns it has achieved.

One of the benefits of an appropriate personal pension is the control you gain over the investment strategy of your fund. If you are not happy with the investment performance of your pension company, you can switch your fund to a different provider – although you will need to look carefully at the costs involved before doing so. Another possible advantage is that the fund you build up will not be affected by any future changes to the state pension.

Men also gain some extra flexibility as far as their pension age is concerned. They cannot take a SERPS pension until age 65, but with an appropriate personal pension they can draw a pension as early as 60. Of course, it has to be borne in mind that if the pension is taken early, then it will be smaller than if it were taken at state pension age.

At retirement, the protected rights fund must be used to buy a special type of annuity to provide your regular pension. Unlike other personal pension plans, none of the fund may be taken as a tax-free cash sum. The annuity must:

- pay the same amount of pension to men and women (normally insurance companies pay different rates to men and women because of their different life expectancies).
- increase at 3% per annum for rebates received in the years up to and including 1996/97 and thereafter the annuity must be linked to the lesser of the retail prices index or 5% per annum.
- provide a 50% spouse's pension after the death of the purchaser, whether or not he or she is married when the annuity is purchased.

The levels of annuity rates at retirement are not guaranteed because they depend largely on long-term interest rates. However, there can also be considerable differences between insurance companies and it is important to shop around to get the best rates. (See Chapter 11 for more detail about annuities.)

2 || *Employers' Pension Schemes*

Many employers run pension schemes for their employees. These arrangements are also described as occupational pension schemes. Currently around 10 million employees – nearly half of the UK's working population – belong to an employer's scheme, while over 7 million pensioners are receiving pensions from them. UK pension funds between them own investments of over £600bn. Until 1988, employers could make membership of a company scheme a condition of employment, but after that employees had to be given the choice of whether they wanted to join or not. However, for most people there is little doubt – becoming a member of an occupational scheme is the best option.

An employer's pension scheme has several advantages over a personal pension. The most important is the contribution which your employer makes to your pension fund. Although you will usually have to contribute a fixed percentage of your pay too, you will receive income tax relief. But not all employers expect you to contribute. Around a quarter of private company schemes are 'non-contributory', which means employers pay the full cost.

Other benefits provided by many company pension schemes include life insurance and spouses' pensions. Schemes may pay an enhanced pension if you are forced to retire early due to ill-health. If you move to another job, you can transfer pension benefits or leave them and receive a deferred pension. These options are examined in more detail in the next chapter.

Eligibility

In the past, employers often set minimum age limits at which employees could join the pension scheme, some as high as 30, or a minimum period of employment of, say, two years. Nowadays, schemes are not so restrictive. The majority allow employees of any age to join their scheme straightaway from age 18 or younger. Some have a maximum age for entry, typically five years before pension age. Many schemes nowadays are open to part-timers, although they may require that employees work more than, say, eight hours per week to be eligible.

Pension scheme membership can no longer be made compulsory but many employers try to encourage the widest participation possible by making membership automatic for eligible employees. Those who do not wish to join can apply to opt out. Other schemes may simply ask you whether you want to join or not.

Some people turn down membership because they do not know how long they will stay with an employer or because they think it will save them money. By not joining, however, you are in effect taking a pay cut because you will be missing out on the contributions your employer would be making to your pension. If you do not choose to join a scheme at the first opportunity, the majority of employers will still allow you to become a member if you change your mind later, though not all are prepared to give you a second chance. Still, if you have turned down membership in the past and now decide it would be a good idea to join, it is worth asking.

When you join a scheme, you will be provided with a booklet which will give you details of all the benefits provided by your scheme. Keep it in a safe place for future reference. If you subsequently have any complaints about your scheme the booklet should explain how the disputes procedure works.

Limits

To encourage companies and their employees to make their own pension provision, there are various tax concessions on both the contributions made to a company scheme and the benefits paid out – up to certain limits.

The most important limits are:

- **Contributions.** There is income tax relief on employee contributions up to a maximum of 15% of earnings.
- **Pension.** The maximum pension is two-thirds of final earnings.
- **Cash sum.** The maximum tax-free cash sum at retirement is one-and-a-half times final salary.
- **Spouse's pension.** The maximum spouse's pension is two-thirds the employee's pension.
- **Earnings.** There is a cap on the level of earnings on which pension contributions and benefits can be based: for example, the maximum for 1998/99 is £87,600. This amount is revalued each year in line with the annual rise in the retail price index. (This cap does not apply to employees in schemes set up before 14 March 1989 or employees joining existing schemes before 1 June 1989.)
- **Tax-free lump sum on death.** The maximum cash sum payable on death before retirement is four times the employee's earnings at the time of death.

How Schemes Work

All pension schemes must operate within the same rules, but they are not all identical. The rules of each scheme are laid down in its trust deed. Some offer more generous benefits than others. There are differences in pension ages, in definitions of earnings and in trustees' discretionary powers. Responsibility for implementing the trust rules, looking after the assets of the scheme and making sure it keeps within the law lies with the trustees. The laws governing pensions have been toughened up considerably since the Robert Maxwell scandal, which saw millions of pounds disappear from the Mirror Group's pension scheme.

Among other things, the Pensions Act 1995 which came into force in April 1997 provided for the appointment of up to one-third of the trustee board from among the scheme's members. This was intended to help to balance the power of the management representatives on the board, although the first duty of all the trustees is in any case to the beneficiaries of the scheme rather than the employer. The Act also introduced a 'minimum funding requirement' to make sure there are enough assets in a pension fund to meet a scheme's liabilities if an employer goes bust.

Types of Pension Scheme

A major difference between schemes lies in the way the size of your pension is determined. There are two main categories: 'final salary' schemes, where the size of the pension is a fixed percentage of your pay at or near retirement, and 'money purchase' schemes, in which the size of your pension fund at retirement determines how much pension can be bought in the form of an annuity.

Final salary schemes

You will generally belong to a final salary scheme if you work in the public sector – the civil service, health service etc – or are employed by a large or medium-sized company. These schemes are also described as 'defined benefit' schemes because the benefit – the pension – is a predetermined percentage of your final pay built up over your years of service.

Most final salary schemes are contracted out of SERPS, which means that employers and employees pay lower rate National Insurance contributions. The difference must be invested in the company pension fund, in addition to the usual contributions. Until April 1997, contracted-out schemes had to provide a guaranteed minimum pension at least as good as the SERPS pension employees would have received. This rule no longer applies to any pension built up since April 1997, although a scheme still has to provide a certain minimum level of pension. It must, for example, provide a build-up in pension of at least one-eightieth of final pay for each year of service, a 50% spouse's pension must be provided and the pension itself must increase by the lesser of the retail prices index or 5% per annum.

- **Contributions.** Employees' contributions are usually a fixed percentage of their pay. The average is around 5%, although amounts can vary from less than 1% to over 6%. Tax relief on contributions means the effective cost to the individual is lower. If you wish to pay in more in order to boost your final pension, you can make additional voluntary contributions (AVCs). (For more details on AVC schemes, see Chapter 6).

    Employers pay the balance of the cost required to provide the guaranteed pension benefits. According to the National Association of Pension Funds, average contributions by employers work out at around 13–14% of pensionable earnings over the long term.

    Actual employer contributions vary considerably because of different benefit levels, different ages of members and investment conditions. A company with a high proportion of older employees, for example, will have to contribute more than one with many young workers. If investment returns have been good and pension funds are in surplus, an employer could pay less or even take a 'contribution holiday' and stop making contributions to the fund. This can be a cause of concern among employees. However, if conditions deteriorate the employer will have to top up the pension fund. The fact that this investment risk is borne by the employers is one of the major advantages of final salary schemes for employees. The new 'minimum fund requirement' brought in by the 1995 Pensions Act will also ensure in future that there is sufficient in a pension fund for it to meet its liabilities.

- **Investment.** The investment of the pension fund is the responsibility of the trustees. Some of the largest companies employ their own investment managers to run portfolios of shares, fixed interest securities and other investments. Medium-sized and smaller companies will normally employ outside fund managers to undertake the investment and administration of the fund within agreed guidelines.

- **Your pension.** With the majority of schemes you build up your pension year by year, each year's membership giving a specific pension entitlement expressed as a fraction of final salary. A typical build-up is for the employee to be entitled to one-sixtieth of final salary for each year of membership of the scheme or service with the employer. This means that an employee will need to have 40 years' service with an employer to build up the maximum pension entitlement of forty-sixtieths, or two-thirds of their final salary.

  Some schemes operate more or less generous pension build-ups. In the public sector, for example, you will often receive one-eightieth of final salary for each year of membership, so the maximum pension is only forty-eightieths, or one half of final salary, after 40 years' service. However, a lump sum is paid in addition to the pension at retirement, which offsets the lower accrual rate.

  The actual pension you receive will depend on your final salary, which you won't know until you are relatively near to retirement. If you still have some years to go it will be affected by future pay rises and promotions. However, for some idea of what you might get see Table 10.

Table 10: How much pension you will get from a final salary scheme

The annual starting pension you can expect for every £1,000 of your final salary assuming no tax free cash is taken

Years in scheme	Pension p.a.	
	60th scheme	80th scheme
	£	£
5	83.30	62.50
10	166.60	125.00
15	250.00	187.50
20	333.33	250.00
25	416.60	312.50
30	500.00	375.00
35	583.30	437.50
40	666.66	500.00

- **What is your final salary?** Another point to bear in mind is that the definition of final salary varies from scheme to scheme, and there are also differences in how much of your salary has been counted for pension purposes. Typically, your 'pensionable earnings', as they are known, are your basic earnings only. Even if you earn regular overtime, bonuses or commission payments, these may not be included.

  In some schemes – known as integrated schemes – the first slice of your earnings is also ignored for pension purposes to take account of the fact that the first part of your retirement income will come from the basic state pension. So your company pension will be smaller than if it was based on your total pay, and your contributions will also be less as a result.

  Then there is the question of which year's pay is considered to be your final salary. It can be your annual pay at retirement, but it is more likely to be calculated on your best year's earnings within a specific period before retirement, commonly five years, or on the average over a longer period, or even the average over the period of your whole pension scheme membership.

  It is useful to check out both of these definitions because

they could influence your decision about whether to go for a promotion near to retirement or, if you have regular overtime earnings which are not counted as part of your pensionable earnings, whether to make additional voluntary pension contributions.

- **Pension increases.** Those who retire from a public sector pension scheme have long enjoyed the benefit of inflation-proofed pensions which have been automatically increased each year in line with the retail price index. Practice among private employers has varied. Some have provided guaranteed increases of 3% p.a., regardless of inflation, some have a good record of providing regular discretionary increases over and above the rate of inflation. Others were less generous.

  The Pensions Act 1995 required all schemes to provide some inflation linking for pensions earned after April 1997. Under limited price indexation, as it is known, pensions must now be increased by the lesser of the rise in the retail prices index or 5% per annum. Some schemes have extended this change to cover pensions built up before April 1997.

- **Death benefits for spouses and unmarried partners.** The vast majority of the schemes provide a lump sum and a spouse's pension in the event of an employee's death before retirement. The lump sum is normally three to four times the employee's annual salary. If someone is not married, they can usually nominate a person to whom they wish the cash to go whether it is a heterosexual or same-sex partner. The nomination forms remain sealed until death.

  A spouse's pension is also payable. This is a particularly valuable benefit because it is usually not just based on the pension entitlement which an employee has built up but is enhanced to include some or all of the pension which he or she could have built up by normal retirement age if death had not intervened. In addition, pensions are often payable to children until they reach age 18 or cease full-time education after 18.

  The typical spouse's pension is 50% of the employee's

benefit, whether death occurs before or after retirement, though it can be as much as two-thirds. It may be reduced if there is a big age gap. Many schemes in the private sector will pay a lower pension if the spouse is more than ten years younger than the employee.

The rules of many schemes stipulate that the spouse's pension can only go to a lawful spouse, although nowadays trustees of private sector schemes often have the discretion to award it to a common-law spouse and may consider a same-sex partner. However, before doing so they may require proof of some financial dependency, for example a joint mortgage which one partner alone could not afford, and evidence that it was a long-term relationship. Nowadays, widowers as well as widows are eligible for spouses' pensions but this is a relatively recent development. Many schemes did not introduce widowers' pensions until 1988 or later, which means they will only apply to any pension entitlement built up after that date. (See Chapter 10 for more details.)

Money purchase schemes

A money purchase scheme provides you at retirement with a 'pot' of money in a pension account which is used to buy your pension. Employers pay a fixed contribution into this account, which is why these arrangements are also described as 'defined contribution' schemes.

Until recently, money purchase schemes were only offered by a minority of employers, but they are becoming increasingly popular because they enable employers to control their costs more than under a final salary scheme. Some employers now operate both types of pension arrangements. A money purchase scheme is offered to younger employees, but they can join the final salary scheme when they are older. Alternatively, the final salary scheme is only kept open for existing members while new employees must use the money purchase scheme.

Money purchase schemes need not be contracted out of SERPS

so in these cases employees will also receive both state pensions at retirement.

- **Contributions.** According to the last annual survey by the National Association of Pension Funds, around a quarter of money purchase schemes are non-contributory and the remainder are roughly evenly split between those requiring fixed contributions from employees and those where contributions vary, with employees often able to choose how much they want to contribute. The average employee contribution is 3.7% of pay. Employees who want to pay extra can make additional voluntary contributions (AVCs). (See Chapter 6 for more details about AVCs.)

    Employer contributions may also be fixed or vary, depending on factors such as age, length of service or the contribution level chosen by the employee. Some employers will match the contribution made by the member. Latest figures show that the overall level of combined employee/employer contributions averages 9.3%. This is considerably less than the average long-term contribution to final salary schemes. However, the National Association of Pension Funds points out that there are a number of reasons for this disparity. Typically, smaller organizations provide money purchase schemes, either because they lack the resources to organize a successful final salary arrangement or because they are in a growth stage. In addition, since the schemes tend not to be contracted out of SERPS, employers still have to pay full National Insurance contributions.

- **Investment.** Investment performance is a crucial factor in determining the size of the pension 'pot' provided by a money purchase scheme. Although each employee will have his or her own individual pension account, investment is undertaken on a collective basis. Employers usually pass the responsibility for investment management to life insurance companies which run such schemes.

    However, employees may be given a choice of investment

funds in some schemes. Where this is available, experience has shown that the best long-term growth is achieved by choosing funds that invest in real assets, such as shares and property. However, as retirement draws near, it is advisable to move investments gradually into fixed interest securities to protect yourself against a fall in the stock market or in interest rates. Some investment managers have automatic fund switching facilities for this purpose.

- **Your pension.** Subject to the maximum permitted pension of two-thirds of final salary, which applies to money purchase as much as to final salary occupational schemes, the amount of pension you can buy at retirement will depend on how much is in your pension account and on annuity rates at the time. An annuity must normally be purchased at retirement in order to provide a regular pension for life. The type of annuity may be dictated by the pension scheme, and by law any pension benefits earned after April 1997 must be used to purchase an annuity which provides limited price indexation, that is, it must increase by 5% per annum of the rate of inflation if less.

  However, an employee may be able to exercise some influence over the type of annuity purchased and also over the insurance company which is used. This opportunity should be taken to ensure that the best possible rates are obtained on the annuity and also that it fits your circumstances. (For more information about annuities, see Chapter 11.)

- **Death benefits for spouses and unmarried partners.** A lump sum of between two and four times an employee's annual salary is payable under most money purchase schemes if death occurs before retirement. If someone is not married a lower sum may be payable. The payment will go to the person nominated by the employee, including a same-sex partner. The nomination forms remain sealed until death.

  In addition the accumulated value of an employee's and employer's contributions may also be paid out on death in service as a lump sum instead of, or as well as, a spouse's pension. Children's pensions are less common with these schemes than with final salary arrangements. Where death occurs after retirement, whether a spouse's pension is provided will often depend on the type of annuity that has been purchased. Many schemes do not insist on an annuity with a spouse's pension attached although this will become obligatory for pensions built up after April 1997.

Group personal pensions

Group personal pensions are a relatively recent innovation. Strictly speaking, they are not occupational pension schemes at all, simply a collection of individual personal pension policies. The main difference from an ordinary personal pension is that instead of paying contributions yourself, they are deducted from your pay and passed to the pension company by your employer.

There are also other differences which are normally to an employee's advantage. For instance, charges may be lower because of the economies of scale. Best of all, employers will normally make a contribution to these plans whereas they are normally more reluctant to contribute to individual employees' contracts.

Group personal pensions are a form of 'money purchase' scheme, so like the occupational arrangements of this type they provide you with a 'pot' of money at retirement in your policy which you will use to buy your pension.

Once a scheme has been set up by an employer it is basically a series of contracts between the employees concerned and the pension provider. It is the responsibility of the pension provider to alert policyholders within three months if an employer should fail to pass on the contributions that have been deducted from employees' pay.

Group personal pensions can be used to contract out of SERPS, but this decision will be left to individuals rather than an employer deciding on behalf of the whole workforce as normally takes place with a company scheme.

● **Contributions.** For employees, the main advantage of group personal pensions over individual policies is that the employer will normally make a contribution to the scheme. The limits on contributions to group schemes are the same as for individual personal pension policies, starting at 17.5% of earnings for employees up to age 35, rising to 40% for employees age 61 and over. (See Chapter 4 for detailed contribution limits.) Employer and employee contributions combined must fall within these limits. Typically, contributions of 5% may be made by both the employer and employed giving a total of 10%. Employees are free to contribute more if they wish to. Some employers will also make provision for contributions from both sides to increase with age. All these contributions are deducted from your pay at source and passed direct to the pension provider.

- **Investment.** Besides the level of contributions, investment performance is vital in determining the ultimate size of your pension 'pot' and thus the pension you can buy at retirement. With a group scheme the employer chooses the pension company, but employees can decide on the investment fund in which they want contributions to be invested.

  There may be a wide range of funds available depending on the pension company. Experience has shown that the best long-term growth is achieved by choosing funds that invest in real assets, such as shares and property. However, as retirement draws near, it is advisable to move investments gradually into fixed interest securities to protect yourself against a fall in the stock market or in interest rates. Some investment managers have automatic fund switching facilities for this purpose. (There is more detail about the investment options within personal pension policies in Chapter 5.)

- **Your pension.** There is no restriction on the amount of pension that can be purchased at retirement with a personal pension plan. The amount is dictated only by size of the pension fund you have built up and the level of annuity rates. In order to get the best annuity rates, you will need to shop around to find which company is offering the most competitive deal. It is not necessary to stick to the company which has provided your pension plan.

You can also choose the type of annuity best suited to your circumstances, although if you have opted out of SERPS that part of your pension fund built up from National Insurance rebates (known as the 'protected rights' fund) can only be used to buy an annuity which pays a pension that increases by the lesser of the retail prices index or 5% per annum and provides a 50% spouse's pension.

3 || *Changing Jobs*

Few people stay with the same employer all their lives nowadays. On average people change jobs around five times during their careers, staying less than 10 years in each position. So the chances are that most people may have to consider what to do with pension benefits accumulated in an ex-employer's pension scheme not once but several times during their working lives.

When you leave an employer it is very important to try and look at your pension options as dispassionately as possible. When people have fallen out with their old employer, or been made redundant against their will, they may wish to shift their pension elsewhere so they can sever all connections with their old company. But there is no point in doing this if it leaves you worse off. There are a variety of factors to consider. Your age, your length of service and the type of scheme you belonged to will influence the situation. If you are moving straight to a new job, you will also need to consider what type of pension arrangement your new employer is offering.

Leaving within Two Years

If you have been a member of an occupational scheme for less than two years, you will often be offered a cash refund of your contributions. If you were contracted out of SERPS through the scheme, the difference between the full and lower rate of National Insurance contribution will be clawed back to buy you back into the state scheme for the period covered by your company scheme membership. A tax charge of 20% deducted from your refunded contributions will offset the tax relief you received. However, this still means most people will receive back slightly more than they paid in as the basic rate tax relief they were given will have been somewhat higher.

This is the only occasion when cash can be paid out of a pension scheme before retirement, except on death. The thought of getting the lump sum may be attractive; but if you are offered the chance of leaving your money invested or transferring your contributions, either may be a better option in the long run. This way you will retain your employer's contributions, which will help to boost your eventual pension at retirement.

If a cash refund is the only option, you should use it to buy your own pension. When you are given a refund of contributions, the period you worked for your employer is deemed to have been 'non-pensionable' so you can set up a personal pension plan and pay in the cash to cover the period you were in the scheme. You can pay your lump sum into a 'single premium' pension plan and it will be boosted by a fresh injection of tax relief. This is possible even if you move to a new job and join another occupational pension scheme immediately.

Group Personal Pension Plans

If you were a member of a group personal plan, you will not have a refund option even if you leave a company within two years and your employer cannot claw back any company contributions when you leave. The plan is yours and you retain ownership of its full value. You can simply continue with the plan if you become self-employed or your new company has no pension scheme. However, you will not be able to do so if your new employer offers an occupational scheme that you wish to join. Most employers are still unwilling to contribute an individual's personal pension plan instead of the company scheme.

Your personal pension provider may allow you to convert your policy to a free-standing additional voluntary contribution contract (FSAVC) so you can continue to make extra savings to top up your company scheme benefits. But find out if there is a cost for making this conversion. Even if there is none, it may still be more cost effective to make your policy paid up and use your new employer's own AVC scheme.

Even if the company scheme is another group personal pension plan, your employer may still refuse to contribute to your policy if it is with another pension provider because of the extra administration involved. As group personal pension schemes become more common, however, a way round this problem may be found.

Nevertheless, if you join another group personal pension scheme, you can still contribute to your previous plan if you can afford it. There is no restriction on the number of personal plans you can have, provided the total combined contributions do not exceed the maximum contribution limit (see page 66). Another option is to transfer your fund to the new personal pension provider. This may be worth considering if the new provider has a better investment performance record, or you discover that there are onerous on-going charges if you have to stop your contributions. But check out possible transfer penalties first.

Group Money Purchase Schemes

Although membership of a money purchase occupational scheme does not give you quite so much flexibility as a group personal pension plan, there will again be a pot of money in the scheme to which you are entitled if you leave the company. You can simply leave this money invested in the scheme to accumulate until your normal pension age. Obviously no further contributions will be made by your previous employer.

However, if you are unhappy with the pension company's investment record, you could consider transferring your fund. Before doing so, you will need to find out whether there are early redemption penalties which would reduce your pension 'pot' and make this option less attractive. If your next employer offers a similar scheme, you may be able to transfer your fund into that arrangement. The other possibility is to place the lump sum into a personal pension or a 'buy-out' bond (more about the pros and cons of these options follow).

Final Salary Schemes

If you have been a member of the scheme for more than two years and therefore do not qualify for a cash refund, you will have up to four options:

- Leave your pension benefits in your former employer's scheme as a deferred pension.
- Take the cash equivalent of these benefits, known as a transfer value, and put it into your new employer's scheme.
- Take a transfer value and invest it in a personal pension.
- Take a transfer value and invest it in an insurance contract known as a Section 32 buy-out bond.

Each option has possible advantages and disadvantages, so you need to consider your position carefully. You do not have to make your decision right away. In fact, if you are not starting a new job immediately, it is probably better to wait until your employment position is clear and then decide. There is no time limit on when you can request a transfer of benefits from a previous employer's scheme, although if you left your job before 1 January 1986, when the right to transfer was introduced, your request can still be turned down.

It is vital to take independent financial advice before you decide in favour of taking a transfer value.

Taking a deferred pension

Leaving your pension with your old employer is the recommended option in most cases nowadays. It means you will eventually receive a pension from your ex-employer at your normal retirement age, based on the number of years you were a member of the scheme and on your final pay at or around the date you left.

In the past, most of your benefits would have been 'frozen' at the level they were when you left. This meant that by the time you reached retirement, maybe 20 or 30 years later, your pension could be worth next to nothing as its value would have been eroded by inflation. However, over the last ten years there have been several improvements in the treatment of deferred benefits which help to ensure that their real value is maintained.

Benefits must now be increased during the period between an employee leaving a company and drawing a pension. Until recently, where a scheme was contracted out of SERPS, the benefits were split into two parts and each was revalued differently. From 1978 that part which replaced SERPS, known as the guaranteed minimum pension, had to be revalued either in line with national average earnings or by a fixed rate, currently 6.25% a year. Typically, public sector schemes have opted for the former method and private sector schemes for the latter. Since April 1997, however, the guaranteed minimum pension has been abolished. Any SERPS replacement benefits built up since that time will now have to be increased in line with 'limited price indexation', that is, by the lesser of the retail prices index or 5% per annum.

Treatment of the remainder of the pension has also varied over the years. In the mid-1980s the Government introduced compulsory increases, but initially this only applied to benefits built up since 1 January 1985. They were also subject to limited price indexation. This revaluation rule was extended at the beginning of the 1990s. Employees who left their schemes on or after 1 January 1991 must now have all their deferred pension increased at least in line with limited price indexation. However, some schemes have been more generous. In the public sector, for example, schemes apply the full rate of increase in the retail price index – there is no 5% limit. Some private sector schemes also follow the same practice.

So people who leave their pension with their previous employer no longer have to worry too much about its value being eroded by inflation. The one snag is that increases in the retail price index have frequently been outpaced by rises in earnings. However, if you move your transfer value to, say, a personal pension plan, there is no guarantee that investment growth will exceed inflation or earnings growth either, and there are other considerations that might make leaving your pension where it is attractive.

Firstly, there is the question of how your pension will be treated when you eventually reach retirement. Once again, public sector schemes have the advantage of providing full inflation proofing for pensions in payment, while some private schemes have a good record of paying regular discretionary increases over and above the rate of inflation. A second consideration is what happens on death before retirement. Some companies continue to provide relatively generous death benefits even to those with deferred pensions.

If you do decide to leave your pension where it is, you may need to review your decision if your ex-employer is taken over by another company which wants to change the arrangements in any way.

Taking a transfer value with you
If you decide to investigate the possibility of taking your pension with you when you leave, you will probably expect the transfer value you get to be roughly equivalent to the contributions you and your employer have paid into the scheme during your period of membership, plus any investment growth that has been added. But that is not how transfer values are calculated.

A transfer value is meant to be the cash equivalent of the deferred pension you would get from the scheme if you left your benefits where they were. So it will be the amount of money which the pension scheme's actuaries calculate would have to invested now at a given rate of interest to accumulate enough money to purchase the deferred pension you would be due at the normal retirement date. Although account will be taken of inflation, up to a maximum of 5%, in arriving at your expected pension, earnings growth is not allowed for. Discretionary increases to pensions in payment may also be excluded.

One of the factors which will be taken into account in working out a transfer value will be long-term interest rates. This is a reason why your transfer values can vary in amount between one request and another. If interest rates go down, your transfer value is likely to go up because a larger sum would have to be invested now to achieve the required result at retirement, and vice versa. Therefore, if you ask for a transfer value quotation, you should also find out how long or under what conditions the figure will remain valid.

You do not have to wait until you have left your job to ask about the size of your transfer value. You can do so at any time and the request should be kept confidential by your pensions department.

Questions to ask your scheme administrator before you decide whether to take a transfer value

- What is the transfer value of my pension?
- Does the scheme provide any discretionary benefits?
- Does the transfer value make allowance for them and will I lose them?
- When my pension comes to be paid, will it increase and by how much?
- Will it be guaranteed to be paid for a minimum period (usually 5 years) if I die early?
- When I die will my dependants get a pension, and how much?
- What benefits will there be if I die before retirement?

Source: NAPF

Putting your transfer value into your new employer's scheme

If you want to join your new employer's pension scheme, you will probably be allowed to bring the transfer value from your old employer's scheme with you (although schemes are not obliged to accept transfer values). But don't expect to receive exactly the same benefits you had in the old scheme. Unless you are moving from one public sector employer to another, you are likely to get less.

You may be offered one of the following:

- Extra years of pensionable service in your new scheme, but probably not as many as you had in your old scheme.
- A fixed annual amount of pension on retirement or death.
- A money purchase pension.

Naturally, one major reason for the variation in what you may receive in the new scheme is that employers may provide different benefits. But even if you were to move between two almost identical schemes and remain on the same salary, you would probably find you were credited with fewer years in your new employer's scheme because of the way the actuary in the new scheme calculates the value of your transferred benefits. He will calculate how much pension the transfer value from your old scheme will provide in the new scheme at normal retirement age. Your anticipated final earnings will also be worked out and it will then be calculated what percentage of these earnings the pension bought with your transfer value represents. This will then be converted back into the 'years of service' normally required in the new scheme to achieve such a level of benefit.

The inconsistency in the calculations arises mainly because the new scheme's actuary will make an allowance for earnings growth in arriving at your anticipated final salary, while the old scheme's actuary has only been able to allow for inflation up to a maximum of 5%. If you start your new job on a substantially higher salary, the gap between pension and anticipated salary is likely to be even greater and hence the number of 'years' you will get in the new scheme even lower. However, if the new scheme offers lower benefits than your old one, it is possible that you could end up with more 'years' in the new scheme.

Even if your transfer value buys you fewer years in your new employer's scheme a transfer may be worthwhile if it is a good scheme, especially if your salary rises faster than anticipated in the calculations. However, if you expect to make further job switches in the future, taking a transfer value every time could prove unwise.

Putting your transfer value into a personal pension

Transferring to a personal pension may have the attraction of giving you your own 'pot' of pension money. However, if you have left a final salary scheme you may be sacrificing the certainty of a guaranteed pension with guaranteed increases to enter a money purchase type scheme which will not pay a guaranteed pension. Any illustrations of future benefits from a personal pension are based on assumed growth rates. The actual results may be very different.

The chief advantage of a personal pension is that you will have more flexibility. You can choose your own investment managers and types of investment funds and decide when to take the pension between the ages of 50 and 75 and what type of annuity you want to buy. If you are not married, you can leave the value of your pension fund to whoever you wish if you die before retirement. But any extra death benefits which you may have received automatically under an employer's scheme, even on a deferred pension, will have to be paid for separately with a personal pension.

If your previous scheme was contracted out of SERPS, part of your transfer value will go into an 'appropriate' personal pension, also known as the 'protected rights' element. As explained in Chapter 2, there are certain restrictions which will affect this part of your pension which will not apply to the rest. For example, you cannot draw a pension on this portion until you are 60 and a unisex annuity must be purchased which provides for a 50% spouse's pension.

Putting your transfer value into a 'buy-out' bond

Buy-out bonds are offered by insurance companies. They can provide a mixture of guaranteed and investment related benefits. Their greatest attraction is normally their potential for providing higher pre-retirement death benefits than a personal pension funded by a transfer value.

With a buy-out bond the insurance company can take over the commitment to provide a guaranteed minimum pension in the case of benefits accumulated up to April 1997. An appropriate amount of the transfer value will usually be invested in a with profits fund for this purpose. Any remaining money can be invested to provide a tax-free cash sum and to buy an annuity of your choice. A higher cash sum may also be available from a buy-out bond than can be taken from a personal pension.

Taking Professional Advice

Even if you do not normally seek financial advice, you should do so when you are considering your pensions options as a result of a job change. Taking advice at this stage could prevent you from making an expensive mistake which might be impossible to correct in the future. Once you have taken a transfer value from an ex-employer's scheme you cannot reverse the decision (unless you were one of the victims of the mis-selling of personal pensions which took place in the late 1980s and early 1990s – see Chapter 4 for more details if you think this may apply to you).

When you are seeking advice on employers' pensions schemes, you must consult a pensions expert. You will need to find an independent financial adviser with relevant expertise. Your employer's own firm of financial advisers may be willing to help. Alternatively, you could consider approaching a consulting actuary with an in-depth knowledge of occupational schemes. You will almost certainly have to pay for this kind of advice, but getting the right advice could end up saving you much more money in the long term.

For more information about where to go for advice, see Appendix II.

Tracing Pensions from Former Employers

As pointed out at the beginning of this chapter, it is very common to have several jobs during your working life nowadays. So unless you have consistently taken transfer values from each of your employers – which may have been impossible before 1 January 1986 – you may well have bits of deferred pension in previous company schemes.

Tracing an old employer yourself may not be easy if the company has been taken over or gone out of business. If you have lost touch with a previous employer, the Pensions Scheme Registry may be able to help you. There is no charge for this service.

The form you will get from the Registry will ask you to give as many details as you can about your former employer's scheme. If there are some you cannot supply it may take longer to provide you with information, but the service generally has a very high success rate in locating previous employers. In theory it only covers pension scheme details available from April 1975, but some schemes have provided information for earlier years, so it is still worth a try even if you were a member of a scheme earlier than 1975.

4 || *Personal Pensions – Who Needs Them?*

Personal pensions are for everyone who works and is not a member of a company pension scheme. It is never too early or too late to invest in a personal pension, and even if you already have a plan it is still worth reading through the next two chapters to ensure you are making the most of it.

Among those eligible for personal pensions are those employees who work for smaller companies which do not have pension schemes or employees who are on short-term contracts with larger employers and not eligible for membership of their company schemes. They are also for the three million self-employed people in the UK and anyone who has some freelance earnings which are not covered by a pension.

Individual pension plans have been around since the 1950s, although personal pension policies in their present form did not become available until 1988 when the Government introduced greater freedom of choice into the pensions area. Unfortunately this situation was exploited by some companies who mis-sold personal pensions to those who would have been better off in employers' pension schemes (see end of chapter for more detail). Nowadays sales of personal pensions are more strictly regulated. However, with over a hundred different plans on sale, it is still important to know what to look for in a personal pension to make sure you get the best deal possible.

This chapter will deal with the general points you need to know about this type of pension plan, and Chapter 5 will cover the main features to look at when choosing a personal pension.

What is a Personal Pension?

A personal pension plan is a convenient way of building up your savings for retirement. It is an arrangement between you and the pension company. You have considerable control. You can decide the investment strategy and how the pension is eventually paid. You do not have to leave your money with the same pension company.

Personal pensions offer various advantages over alternative forms of saving. Besides tax concessions, they allow you to insure your savings so they will continue even if you suffer disability, they offer the opportunity to buy cheap life insurance, and when you reach retirement they provide an income guaranteed for life.

The Tax Advantages

The strongest argument for saving for your retirement through a personal pension plan are the tax advantages:

- **Income tax relief.** When you pay into your pension plan you will receive income tax relief on your contributions. Employees pay contributions net of basic rate tax. The tax is then reclaimed by your pension company, boosting your investment by around a third. Any higher rate tax relief due is reclaimed via your tax return. Similarly, the self-employed must pay the full contribution but they gain the tax relief when they submit their annual tax return, leading to a reduction in their tax bill.
- **Tax concessions on investments.** Pension funds can no longer reclaim tax paid on UK share dividends, but all other income from overseas shares, fixed interest securities and property is tax free. No capital gains tax is payable either.
- **Tax free cash.** At retirement, you can take a tax-free lump sum of up to 25% from your pension fund.
- **Inheritance tax.** If you die before retirement, or before purchasing a pension annuity, the value of your pension fund can be paid to your beneficiaries free of inheritance tax if it is written in trust.

Who can take out a Personal Pension?

Employees

An employee may wish to take out a personal pension for a number of reasons:

- *For opting out of the state earnings related pension scheme (SERPS).* Employees who do not belong to a company pension scheme or whose scheme is not contracted out of SERPS can opt out of the state scheme using a personal pension plan. Part of their National Insurance contributions plus part of their employers' contributions will then be rebated by the DSS and paid directly into the pension of their choice. They will also receive tax relief on their own contributions. A plan financed by National Insurance rebates is an 'appropriate' personal pension and the fund which accumulates is known as the 'protected rights fund'.

  If investment returns are good, there is the possibility of ending up with a better income from a personal pension than the SERPS equivalent, but this is not guaranteed. You will need to pay extra contributions if you want to increase your chances of getting a better pension.

  Opting out of SERPS may not be a wise decision for all employees. (See Chapter 2 for more information on this point.) It is important to ask an independent financial adviser or pension company for advice on this matter.

- *For topping up the state pension.* Even if you decide to remain in SERPS, the pension you will get is unlikely to meet all your needs in retirement. So it is still advisable to make your own savings in a personal pension. In future, pensions paid under SERPS will be 20% of your lifetime's earnings. So any time spent out of the labour market will reduce your eventual entitlement. Women who have taken time out to bring up a family will have received protection for their basic state pension entitlement, but this protection does not cover SERPS.

  Having your own personal pension will not only ensure you have extra retirement income, it will also give you other benefits and greater flexibility. For example, you can take part of your pension as a tax-free lump sum when you retire. You can also start drawing your pension before state pension age if you wish. A personal pension can be taken at any age between 50 and 75.

● *As a substitute for a company pension scheme.* Some employers do not allow employees to join the company scheme immediately or until they reach a certain age, sometimes as late as 30. While they are waiting, employees should start a personal pension so they do not lose any valuable time. It is cheaper to buy extra pension when you are young than to make up for it later with AVCs.

Once they are offered membership of a company scheme, employees should not normally turn down the opportunity. If for some reason they do, they will need to set up a personal pension instead, otherwise they will have a major gap in their pension provision. The problem is that by doing this they will invariably lose out on the contribution their employer would have made to the group scheme on their behalf. It is very rare for employers to make the same contribution to an employee's own personal pension, unless the company's own scheme is a group personal pension arrangement in which case an employer may well consider paying into a new employee's existing personal pension plan instead.

● *For investing a transfer value from a previous company pension scheme.* Do not consider investing a transfer value from a company scheme in a personal pension plan unless you are sure you would not be better off leaving your fund where it is or transferring it to a new employer. With both these options future increases in your fund are guaranteed, which is not the case with a personal pension plan. However, if these alternatives are not attractive or you are given a refund of your contributions because you have been a member of a company scheme for less than two years, then a personal pension plan can be used. Always seek financial advice before considering a transfer of benefits.

The self-employed

If you are self-employed a personal pension is vital. The basic state retirement pension is the only state pension to which you will be entitled unless at some stage during your working life you were an employed person and paid contributions towards a SERPS pension.

It is easy to put off thinking about a pension when you are first self-employed and money is short. However, try investing something at this stage even if you start on the minimum premium of £20 per month. Not only is something better than nothing, but these contributions will have longer to grow. Any delay in starting your pension provision is surprisingly expensive (see Introduction). Moreover, as a self-employed person, one of the attractions of pension contributions is that they help to reduce your tax bills. If you really are unable to save anything, you will be able to make up for it later. Under personal pension rules, you can make up for current shortfalls in your contributions over the coming six years. (See Chapter 6 for more detail.)

Another reason why some self-employed people do not make adequate pension provision is they assume they will be able to sell their business or other assets when they reach retirement and live off the proceeds. This is a dangerous strategy because there is no guarantee that a business will still be marketable in the future and the value of other assets could also be affected by recessions, technological development or unforeseen changes in fashion. A personal pension can provide a more predictable retirement income.

Contribution Limits

There are restrictions on how much you can invest in a personal pension plan in each tax year, although most people do not need to worry because their contributions are rarely anywhere near the maximum. The limits are related to your age at the beginning of the tax year and the size of your income, as Table 11 shows. They are expressed as a percentage of your 'net relevant earnings'. These earnings equate to your gross annual pay if you are an employee. For the self-employed, they are basically your profits less deductible business expenses.

There are two other restrictions. If you do not have any earnings you cannot contribute to your pension plan, which is a nuisance if you stop work for a period and could afford to continue paying out of savings. The other is that a ceiling is imposed on the amount of net relevant earnings to which the contributions apply – £87,600 for the 1998/99 tax year – which is increased each year in line with the rise in the retail price index. So there is a monetary limit to the contributions you may pay. For example, the maximum annual contribution someone in their late forties can make is £21,900.

Table 11: Personal Pension contribution limits

Age at 6 April	Maximum contribution payable in tax year (% of net relevant earnings)
Up to 35	17.5%
36–45	20.0%
46–50	25.0%
51–55	30.0%
56–60	35.0%
61 and over	40.0%

Death Benefits

If you die before reaching retirement, your pension may be treated as two parts. Any part which has been financed from National Insurance rebates where you have opted out of SERPS will provide a 50% spouse's pension, provided your spouse is aged 45 or over or if younger has dependent children. The pension fund built up from your own contributions will normally be paid into your estate for your spouse or other beneficiaries. A spouse's pension is not provided automatically, so it will be up to your spouse or other beneficiaries to decide what to do with the lump sum.

Remember that as time goes on your pension fund is likely to become a very substantial investment, so it is important to make sure that tax is not incurred unnecessarily if you die early, especially if you have dependants. You can prevent this happening by writing your policy 'in trust'. This will ensure that the proceeds are not included in your estate for inheritance tax purposes and that your beneficiaries get immediate access to the money.

Life Cover

In the early years, the value of your pension policy is not likely to be great. So unless your spouse or partner has adequate financial resources, you should consider taking out extra life insurance. You can use part of your pension contribution allowance for this purpose. Up to 5% of your contribution limit can be used to buy life insurance. The advantage of buying life cover in this way is that you will get income tax relief on your premiums, unlike normal life insurance policies on which no tax relief is given.

The life insurance available in conjunction with pension policies is 'term insurance'. It pays out a lump sum if you die before retirement, but there is no savings element: if you survive you won't receive anything. You can buy this life insurance from your pension provider, but you do not have to. It may be cheaper to buy a separate policy elsewhere. Some pension providers will only sell cover to people who have one of their pension policies, but other insurers sell it independently.

If you do buy the cover, remember to put these benefits 'in trust'. This way the proceeds can pass straight to your beneficiaries and not to your estate, where they may become liable to inheritance tax. It will also help speed up the payment.

Waiver of Premium

Although it is important to ensure that you have adequate life insurance, you are more likely to suffer a long-term illness than to die before you reach retirement, leaving a nasty gap in your pension provision. It is well worth considering paying a small extra charge for the waiver of premium benefit which most personal pension providers offer. This benefit ensures that the contributions to your pension plan are maintained on your behalf by your pension provider for as long as you cannot work due to disability. The waiver normally starts after you have been sick or disabled continuously for three to six months and the deduction to pay for it typically ranges between 2% and 4% of your premiums. Some pension companies vary the cost according to your age and your occupation.

If you want to take up this option, it should ideally form part of your deliberations when you are considering your choice of pension plans as there are differences in individual providers' waiver of contribution facilities; most significantly in how they define disability. Only if you satisfy their definition will the waiver of premium come into force.

There are three main definitions:

- Inability to carry out your own occupation.
- Inability to carry out your own occupation or one for which you are suited by education or training.
- Inability to do any kind of work.

Some companies tailor the definition to your occupation. You should steer clear of providers which restrict benefits to the final category, as this requires a very extensive degree of disablement.

Benefits from Personal Pension Policies

The main reason for setting up a personal pension plan is to ensure you have an adequate income in retirement. Unlike company schemes, there is no restriction on how large that income can be. The amount will depend purely on how large a fund you have managed to accumulate and annuity rates at the time you retire. (Annuities are discussed in more detail in Chapter 11.)

However, there is a limit on how much tax-free cash you can take at retirement. That limit is 25% of your pension fund, excluding any part of the fund which consists of 'protected rights', i.e. has been built up from SERPS National Insurance rebates; no part of this can be taken in cash. You can start taking benefits from a personal pension policy any time between the ages of 50 and 75 and you don't actually need to have retired to do so. However, you do have to wait until the normal state pension age before you can take a pension from the 'protected rights' portion of your policy.

Retirement Annuities

If you took out your pension plan before 1 July 1988, you will have what is known as a 'retirement annuity' or 'Section 226' policy. Although no one was able to take out a new retirement annuity after that date, there is nothing to stop existing policyholders continuing or increasing their contributions to these policies.

There are several differences between the old-style policies and personal pensions. One is that the limits on contributions as a percentage of earnings are lower under retirement annuities for those aged over 36 and over. However, the earnings cap which limits the monetary amount which can be contributed to a personal pension does not apply.

Table 12: Retirement annuity contribution limits

Age on 6 April	*Maximum pension contribution in tax year (% of net relevant earnings)*
Up to 50	17.5%
51–55	20.0%
56–60	22.5%
61 or over	27.5%

Holders of retirement annuities can also contribute to personal pension policies provided the combined savings they are making in both policies do not exceed the limit for personal pension contributions.

Other distinctions between the two types of contracts are that retirement annuities cannot be used for contracting out of SERPS or accept transfer values from company pension schemes.

Practice is also different with regard to death benefits. Under a personal pension contract, the full value of the fund will normally be paid into the policyholder's estate in the event of death before retirement. When retirement annuities were being sold, this provision was less common. It was more usual for a return of premiums plus a modest rate of interest to be paid on death. Some companies gave investors the option of a death benefit restricted to a return of premiums only with the promise of higher pension at retirement instead.

Anybody who still has a retirement annuity contract should check out the provision on death and then compare the death benefit and the current value of their fund. The gap could be considerable. It is unlikely that your insurer would be willing to convert such a contract to a return of fund basis at no cost, so it may be cheaper to take out extra life insurance to cover the possible loss. Further differences between a retirement annuity and a personal pension arise at retirement. For example, benefits from a retirement annuity cannot be taken until age 60. There is also a difference in the way the tax-free lump sum is calculated.

Holders of the old-style policies are not restricted by these rules as they can convert their contracts into personal pensions at any time, but once this has been done the switch cannot be reversed. (The pros and cons of switching to a personal pension at retirement are discussed in Chapter 11.)

The Mis-selling of Personal Pensions

If you were sold a personal pension during the late 1980s and early 1990s, and you fell into one of the following categories, it is possible that you were wrongly advised:

- You were an employee who opted out of a company scheme to take out a personal pension.
- You took a transfer value from your company scheme and placed it in a personal pension.
- You did not join a company scheme because you were sold a personal pension.

It is also possible that some people who opted out of SERPS were given the wrong advice because their incomes were too low and they were too old to benefit.

If you were in any of these categories you should by now have been contacted by your pension company. The Government and financial regulators have told companies and financial advisers that they must provide victims of mis-selling with compensation to put them back in the position in which they would have been if they had not taken out a personal pension. This will involve either arranging for you to be reinstated in your pension scheme or topping up your personal pension.

If you have not been contacted or you have lost touch with your pension provider and think you might have a case, contact your pension company or the Financial Services Authority which regulates the companies and financial advisers involved. The FSA's Consumer Helpline is 0845 6061234.

5 ‖ *Choosing a Personal Pension*

Deciding you need a personal pension is easy; finding the right plan is more difficult. Charges differ, performance differs, some plans are more flexible than others. What's more pension companies are constantly updating their plans, so whenever you consider topping up your pension contributions it is advisable to check whether you could get better terms elsewhere. There is no restriction on the number of pension plans you have, provided your contributions don't exceed the limits.

There are a variety of considerations to take into account when you choose a personal pension plan. The main factors are:

- **Type of plan.** Which investment approach suits your circumstances best?
- **Performance.** Does the pension company have a good investment record?
- **Charging structures.** How much of your savings will be absorbed in charges?
- **Flexibility.** How well will a plan adapt to possible changes in your future circumstances?
- **Payments.** Would it be better to make regular savings or pay in lump sums?

If you turn to a financial adviser for help, bear in mind that his or her status will influence the advice you will be given. Unless you consult an independent financial adviser, who can deal with any pension company, then you will only be informed about one company's products. Even an independent financial adviser may not recommend a company which does not pay sales commission, unless you are prepared to pay a fee for advice. (More about where to get advice in Chapter 12.) So the more you know yourself the better.

Fortunately, choosing a personal pension is not a once-and-for-all decision. You can stop contributing to one plan and start putting your savings into another, or you can even move your existing pension fund to another company if you are not satisfied. However, both alternatives can be a costly. Getting it right in the first place is best.

Which Type of Pension Policy?

There are dozens of different personal pension policies offered by companies as diverse as the Prudential, the Halifax, Marks & Spencer and Virgin Direct. One of the main distinguishing features of different companies' pension plans is the type of investment funds they offer, although some companies provide a choice of different funds within one contract. So before you choose a pension policy, you will need to decide which type of fund you want. In other words, you must consider which type of fund is likely to give you the best results over the period left until your retirement. With personal pensions, investment growth plays a vital role in determining the size of your fund at retirement and this in turn will determine how much pension you can buy.

Here are some points to bear in mind when making your choice; they are also illustrated in Table 13 by the annual performance figures for shares and building society accounts:

- Over the long term, real assets such as shares and property produce the best returns and protection against inflation.
- Shares, and to a lesser extent property, can fluctuate significantly in value over short periods.
- Cash deposits give steady returns and do not suffer variations in capital value, but over all but the shortest terms have historically produced the worst returns.

Table 13: Shares versus building society accounts: year-on-year returns since 1978

	% Growth in share prices	% Gross return on building society account
1997	25	3
1996	12	3
1995	20	4
1994	–10	4
1993	20	4
1992	14	6
1991	16	8
1990	–12	11
1989	35	10
1988	5	7
1987	2	7
1986	19	8
1985	15	10
1984	23	9
1983	23	8
1982	22	9
1981	7	10
1980	27	11
1979	4	10
1978	3	7

Source. Datastream/ICV

Bearing these points in mind, experts recommend that the longer the time until your retirement the more you should invest in real assets. As you get nearer to taking your pension you can shift your fund gradually into safer investments, such as fixed interest securities and deposits. Alternatively, there are funds which provide more stable returns by holding a mixture of assets. Here are the main types of funds to consider depending on how long you have until retirement. However, your attitude to risk may also influence your choice.

More Than Ten Years to Retirement

Unit linked equity funds

Many pension companies offer unit linked pension policies which give savers access to funds which specialize in UK shares or in the shares of the world's other leading stock markets in the United States, Japan and Europe. An international equity fund may also be available which spreads your money across various overseas stock markets.

Investing in shares involves risk, but these funds contain the shares of many companies which helps to spread your risk. They are usually managed by professional investment managers who buy shares in businesses which they believe will do well and sell them when they feel they have reached their potential. Investing in overseas share funds can increase risk because there is the added danger of currency fluctuations, but there is also the possibility of gaining higher returns if other countries' economies are growing faster than the UK economy.

Some equity funds are run as index trackers. They invest in those shares which make up a stock market index, such as the FT-SE 100 Index, which measures the share price movements of the UK's 100 largest companies, or the FT-SE All Share Index, which covers shares of companies of different sizes. By tracking these indices they ensure that their performance matches that of the stock market.

Your pension contributions will buy 'units' in these investment funds and the price of the units will fluctuate in line with the market value of the fund's assets. This means that if investment conditions are poor your policy may go down, but when markets rise you will receive the full benefit of any gains.

Over ten years or more unit linked equity funds should produce the best results, but as you near retirement you should consider switching your investments to a more secure fund, such as a fixed interest or deposit fund. Some companies offer automatic switching facilities for this purpose.

Unit and investment trusts

In recent years a number of unit and investment trust groups have started offering personal pensions linked to their trusts, invested mainly in UK and overseas shares. As well as offering general UK and international trusts, they also have more specialist funds investing in the shares of small companies, for example, or in the stock markets of emerging countries. Some plans offer a managed option which includes a selection of their trusts. Index tracker trusts may also be available.

Generally speaking, these plans work much like unit linked policies. Your pension contributions buy units in your chosen unit trust or shares in an investment trust and the value of your pension fund fluctuates in line with the fortunes of these trusts. In the case of unit trusts, price movements reflect variations in asset values, but investment trusts are somewhat more complicated as their share prices reflect demand for the trusts as well as asset value movements.

The risks and rewards tend to be greater than those associated with unit linked funds, so this type of pension plan is usually recommended for those with some other form of pension provision.

Around Ten Years to Retirement

Unit linked managed funds

These are popular funds in most unit linked personal pension plans because they invest in a mixture of equities, property, fixed interest securities and cash. This combination gives the potential for capital growth through the equity and property investments, with the bonds and cash providing an element of stability.

In theory, the investment managers can change the asset mix to meet changing investment circumstances. In practice, they are likely to keep the majority of the portfolio in shares. However, some companies offer a choice of different types of managed funds, such as 'cautious' and 'adventurous', generally reflecting the fact that the funds have more or less invested in shares. Your pension contributions will buy units in the managed fund, which will fluctuate in price in line with the market value of the fund's investments. So they can go down as well as up in value. Although the fluctuations are not likely to be as great as those in a fund which invests in shares only, it may still be advisable to switch to a more secure fund, such as a pure fixed interest or deposit fund near to retirement.

With profits funds

With profits pensions have been offered by insurance companies since the 1950s. They are often regarded as a 'halfway house' between investing in high risk assets, such as shares, and low risk deposits. They aim to produce capital growth while at the same time providing a considerable degree of security.

Under the with profits system, your savings are put into funds which hold a mixture of UK and overseas shares, property, fixed interest securities and deposits. The profits from these investments are added to your policy in the form of regular and additional bonuses which are calculated in a way designed to smooth out the fluctuations in investment markets. To achieve steady returns, past performance and possible future returns are both taken into account when bonus levels are decided on. After a particularly good period, therefore, some profits will be held back so that bonuses can be cushioned when markets turn down again. At the end of the investment term, when you want to start to take your pension, a final bonus will normally be added to make up for the growth in the fund's investments that has not been reflected in the regular bonus additions.

That is the basic with profits approach; how it works in practice varies between insurance companies and according to whether you have a 'traditional' or 'unitized' with profits contract. Broadly, the two types work as follows:

- **Traditional with profits policies.** Typically, these policies provide a guaranteed basic benefit, plus two tiers of bonuses – a low guaranteed bonus rate calculated on the basic benefit, plus a higher bonus which is applied to the sum of the attaching bonuses. A final bonus is normally added when the policy matures, and may account for a significant part of the final value.

- **Unitized with profits policies.** Nowadays most with profits policies are 'unitized', which means that your savings buy units in the with profits fund. The price of the units will normally increase in line with the declared bonus rate, although some companies have a fixed unit price and add bonuses in the form of extra units. A guaranteed minimum bonus rate may be offered, but normally a single annual rate is declared which is on a par with long-term interest rates. A final bonus may be added when the policy matures to reflect increases in capital values.

A major attraction of with profits policies are the guarantees provided – under traditional policies bonuses once declared cannot be taken away, while with unitized policies unit prices are guaranteed not to fall. However, prospective investors should ask whether bonuses are affected if retirement takes place earlier than expected. With a traditional policy, your final bonus may be affected. With a unitized policy, insurers often retain the right to impose a market value adjustment factor if the investments markets have dropped and growth within the fund does not justify the bonus rate declared.

Five Years or less to Retirement

As you get close to retirement, a more cautious approach to investment is generally advisable, whether you are considering new savings or have built up your savings in an equity fund. However, it may depend partly on what other types of pension provision you have and whether you are planning to buy an annuity at retirement to provide a regular pension or take the income drawdown approach (see Chapter 11 for more detail on these choices).

If you have already built up a reasonable level of pension in a final salary company pension scheme in a previous job, you may be happy to be more adventurous. If not, and you are intending to buy an annuity in a few years time, it may be wiser to minimize your risk by opting for secure funds. Your main choices are:

Cash or deposit funds
These funds are similar to building society accounts. The value of your savings cannot fall and you will receive tax-free interest. Because of the large size of the funds, managers are able to invest in bulk in money market deposits in order to obtain competitive rates of interest.

Fixed interest funds
These funds invest in a mixture of government securities, local authority stock and corporate bonds and receive interest on this stock. The price of the funds can fluctuate, although variations are not likely to be as great as those in equity funds. The main influence on prices of fixed interest securities is the general level of interest rates. The advantage for investors as they approach retirement is that variations in fixed interest funds tend to mirror movements in annuity prices particularly if the fund specializes in long-dated gilts. In other words, if interest rates go down, the prices of fixed interest stock rise, which increases fund values. This gives the investor more money to buy a larger annuity which can offset the fall in income and vice versa.

Guaranteed or protected equity funds
These funds are designed to give you the best of both worlds – the possibility of enjoying stock market growth without the danger of losing money if the market goes down. This is achieved by investing part of the fund in financial derivatives. Stock market growth is usually linked to movements in the FT-SE 100 Index. It will reflect gains in share prices, but there will usually be no benefit from the income paid on the shares which you would get in an ordinary equity fund. Limited amounts of growth may be 'locked in' to the fund at regular intervals.

Investment Performance

Unless you invest your savings in an index tracker fund, which will produce roughly the same results whichever company's pension plan you choose (though charges may differ), the next consideration after deciding on the type of fund you want is potential investment performance. Surveys of past performance show that the variations in the results achieved by different companies can be extremely wide.

Unfortunately, there is no infallible way of knowing which company is going to achieve the best investment performance in the future. Most financial advisers attach considerable value to past performance tables when assessing how companies might do in years to come, although it must be remembered that 'past results are no guarantee of future performance'.

Investors can examine past performance results for themselves by referring to the surveys of past results and fund performance which are published regularly in magazines and periodicals such as *Money Management* and *Life & Pensions Moneyfacts* (these publications should be available via a public library; if not, see Appendix 2 for contact details). However, when examining such information it is important to take various factors into account:

- **With profit plans.** The performance of these contracts is the most difficult to assess because current bonuses do not necessarily reflect current investment performance. A company may be able to afford to pay large bonuses now as a result of too much caution, or meanness, in the past. So look into the consistency of a company's results and at the performance of its other investment funds, if possible, for a more up-to-date picture.

    Another factor to take into account is a company's financial strength; the stronger it is, the greater its ability to smooth out investment returns. It will also have more investment freedom. Because equities and property have provided higher long-term returns historically than fixed interest securities and deposits, it may also be useful to look at the investment strategy of a company's with profit fund (available in its with profits guide).

- **Unit linked plans.** A variety of investment funds are available in most unit linked pension policies. The best results are often produced by the most specialist funds, but so are the worst. Don't be tempted to invest your pension contributions in a highly specialist fund which may be top of the performance tables but could be very high risk. It is also worth examining the performance of a company's whole range of equity funds to make sure its talents are not concentrated in just one area.

  If you are interested in the managed fund, check out the investment strategy – how much is in equities, for example. Find out what opportunities you have to switch to more secure funds as you near retirement.

- **Unit and investment trust plans.** Most of the pension plans of this type have not been around long enough to have past performance records. However, many of the unit and investment trusts in which they invest have, and there is ample performance information about these funds over long and short terms. Once again, beware of assuming that a top performing specialist fund will continue to produce the best results in future. Take a good look at a manager's whole range of funds to ensure there is consistency.

Charges

The charges deducted from your pension contributions are an important factor in determining the value of your pension fund at retirement. Some of the deductions may sound fairly harmless, but high charges can have a devastating effect. With the most expensive policies they can reduce the final value of your fund by over 20%. Naturally, pension companies have to charge you something to cover their overheads and their costs, which include paying the person who sells you the policy be it a telephone operator or a financial adviser. But nobody wants to pay excessive charges. Fortunately, nowadays, it is easier to assess the impact of deductions.

The way charges are deducted from pension policies varies between companies and also according to the type of contract chosen. They may include:

- **An initial charge**, usually 5%. This is usually covered by the 'bid/offer' spread: the difference between the (offer) price you pay for units every time you pay a contribution and the (bid) price you get for your units when your pension fund is transferred or matures.
- **A policy fee.** This may be taken from your policy each month or every time you pay a premium. It may only be a couple of pounds, but it will often increase over time. Increases may be linked to rises in the retail price index or national average earnings index.
- **Allocation rate.** The percentage of each premium which is allocated to buy units in your chosen investment fund after the initial charge has been deducted. The remainder covers other costs. With some plans, charges are spread evenly over the term, so allocation rates remain steady throughout at, say, 97%, while other plans have a lower allocation rate of, say, 63% during the early months or years to cover heavier initial costs, later increasing to, say, 102%. The former method tends to produce higher early transfer values and the latter higher maturity values. Allocation rates may also vary according to the term of the policy and the size of the contribution.
- **Annual charge.** This charge is deducted from the fund mainly to cover the cost of investment management. It can range from 0.5% to 1.5% per year and may increase in the future.
- **Capital units.** These are special units which may be allocated in the early years of a policy and have higher annual charges than normal, sometimes as high as 8% p.a. These charges apply to these units for the whole policy term.

It is difficult for savers to work out how much all the charges mount up to. However, nowadays you can see how they affect your pension in the 'key features' document that all pension companies must provide to prospective policyholders.

Key Feature Documents

These documents provide you with some basic information about your policy and the risks involved. They also show the impact of all charges on your pension and how much has been paid to the person who has sold you the policy.

A standard table is included, an example of which is given in Table 14. It will show the premiums to be paid, the actual deductions which will be made, the 'effect of deductions' – assuming the money invested will grow over time – and what your eventual fund might amount to. These figures are given each year for the first five years and every five years after that to the end of the policy. In their documents all companies must use the same standard assumptions about investment returns. For pension policies, the rate of investment growth used in the key features deductions table is 9%. Another piece of information given about the effect of charges over the whole policy term is known as the 'reduction in yield'. This shows how the charges will bring down the investment growth on the policy. The wider the difference between the before and after investment growth, the more expensive the policy.

To complete the picture, the 'cost of advice' is shown as a separate item although it is included in the total deductions. For independent financial advisers (IFAs) this will normally be the amount of commission they receive from the pension company, although some may take no commission and charge the investor a fee instead. Company representatives may be paid by a combination of salary, bonus and commission, and may have other non-cash benefits such as office services provided by the company whose products they sell. However, to allow a fair comparison with the commission received by IFAs, all these things have to be valued and also shown in the key features document as a cash sum for the 'cost of advice'.

Table 14: Example of a key features illustration table for a personal pension, showing deductions and transfer values for a personal pension taken out by a man aged 30, paying a gross monthly premium of £100.

WARNING – If you retire or transfer to another pension scheme during the early years you could get back less than has been paid in.

The last two columns assume that investments will grow at 9% a year.

At end of year	Total paid in to date	Total actual deductions to date	Effect of deductions to date	What the transfer value might be
The Early Years				
	£	£	£	£
1	1200	145	145	1110
2	2400	300	314	2310
3	3600	470	512	3610
4	4800	653	741	5010
5	6000	851	1000	6520
The Later Years				
10	12000	2110	3030	16000
15	18000	3960	6850	30000
20	24000	6660	13700	50600
25	30000	10500	25700	80700
30	36000	16300	46400	125000
At age 65	42000	24600	81200	190000

What are the deductions for?

- The deductions include the cost of commission, expenses and charges.
- The last line in the table shows that over the full term of the plan, the effect of the total deductions could amount to £81,200.
- Putting it another way, this would have the same effect as bringing the investment growth used from 9% a year down to 7.4%.

Source: Norwich Union

It is important to know how one company's charges compare with those of others offering similar pension policies. Figures need to be compared at different stages of the policy. A plan which has low deductions after five years may not necessarily be the one with the lowest deductions or reduction in yield at the end of the term. Some companies now offer two versions of their plans, one with high transfer values in the early years and one with higher maturity values. To find out how the charges of all companies compare you will need to look at pension surveys published in periodicals such as *Money Management*.

Charges must always be weighed against potential returns. Differences in investment results may have a much bigger effect on policy values than differences in charges. In other words, you will not necessarily gain by taking out a cheap plan if it produces poor results. The best choice may well be a plan with a reasonable level of charges offered by a company which has shown it can produce consistently good performance results.

Flexibility

Most people take out regular premium pension plans with the intention of continuing to save until their chosen retirement age; but circumstances may change, so it is always advisable to find out before you start a policy what might happen if you can no longer maintain contributions.

Points to note include:

- **Making a policy 'paid up'.** Find out when a pension acquires a 'paid up' value – that is, when you can stop making contributions without losing all your savings. Some policies require you to have built up a fund of a certain amount, such as £500, or to have made contributions for a period of, say, one or two years.
- **The charging structure.** Heavy initial charges may mean your policy has little value if you stop paying contributions in the early years. Unless you are confident of maintaining contributions, choose a policy which distributes charges more evenly.
- **Stopping and starting premiums.** Check whether there are any restrictions on how long you can stop paying contributions without being penalized. Some policies offer limited 'premium

holidays' only of, say, two years. If you fail to restart the policy within the period, you will be charged extra when you do eventually resume saving.

- **Portability.** Ask whether the policy can be converted to another form of pension policy, such as a free-standing AVC, at no extra cost.
- **Transfer values.** If you want to switch your pension fund to another provider, will you be penalized?

Regular versus Single Premium Policies

Pension plans are normally thought of as a form of regular saving. However, contributions can also be made in the form of one-off investments or single premiums starting at around £500. This method of payment is a particularly useful means of topping up your pension if you receive a lump sum, or you don't want to commit yourself to making regular contributions over a fixed period. You will still receive tax relief as you do on regular contributions.

The main advantage of the single premium is that the deductions are lower because the amount of commission paid to salesmen is less. There is also no danger of any financial loss if you make no further contributions. Another benefit is that you are not tied to one type of pension contract or investment manager. You can invest in different types of policies with different companies.

A potential drawback of the single premium, however, is that there is less savings discipline involved. Having regular savings deducted from a bank account every month makes it easier for many people to save. Also, with single premiums there is a greater possibility of getting your investment timing wrong – for example, investing when shares are most expensive. With regular premiums there is no need to worry about timing, because your premiums will be invested when investment conditions are good and bad so you get the benefit of 'pound cost averaging' which brings down the average price at which you buy investments in your pension fund. Some providers now have regular premium policies with charging structures the same as single premium policies. The alternative is to have a basic regular premium policy and add single premiums when you have extra funds available.

Self-Invested Personal Pensions

Most people's needs can be met by ordinary personal pension plans, at least for most of their working lives. However, if you have built up a very large investment in your pension, perhaps spread across more than one pension provider, then you could consider opening or transferring existing funds to a self invested personal pension (SIPP). This may be particularly worthwhile if you are considering deferring the purchase of an annuity and taking income withdrawals from your fund (see Chapter 11 for more detail).

The advantage of a SIPP is that you have much greater investment freedom than with ordinary pension plans, where you are normally restricted to one fund manager. It allows you to switch between investments without having to transfer your whole policy. The administration is undertaken by an insurance company, but your choice of investments is completely open. Within your fund you can include UK shares, bonds and gilts, overseas shares, and commercial property or any unit or investment trust, insurance company fund or deposit account. A SIPP can be attractive to business partnerships, who can take out a group policy and use their fund to buy new business premises, though they will have to lease them back from the fund on a commercial basis.

However, a full SIPP is only feasible for substantial investors because of the extra expenses involved. These may include the cost of employing an investment adviser or stockbroker because, while you could make the investment decisions yourself, most people do not have the time or necessary expertise. Some schemes, known as hybrid SIPPs, may be somewhat cheaper. They are a halfway house between a managed and self invested plan, usually requiring a minimum contribution each year to the insurance company's own funds while other money can be invested elsewhere.

6 || *Topping up an Inadequate Pension*

Once you become a member of a company scheme or take out a personal pension, you may feel that the matter is taken care of. However, if you want to be sure of enjoying the best retirement you possibly can, you will need to review your pension arrangements regularly. There will almost certainly be scope for you to top up your benefits either within a pension scheme or by making other tax efficient savings. If you are hoping to retire early, making extra savings for your retirement is particularly important.

Employees in company pension schemes who will not have achieved the maximum permitted pension of two-thirds of final salary at retirement – and very few employees do – can make additional voluntary contributions (AVCs), or if you belong to a public sector scheme you may be able to buy 'added years'. All pension schemes must offer members the facility to make AVCs. It is also possible to set up your own scheme outside the company through a 'free standing' AVC or FSAVC. If you have a personal pension extra contributions can also be made to make up for shortfalls in contributions in the past.

However, if you don't want to tie all your savings up in a pension, there are other savings schemes to consider which are also tax efficient and give you greater flexibility. In this chapter, details are given about AVCs, topping up your personal pension and other savings products worth your consideration which will help to make your retirement more comfortable.

Additional Voluntary Contributions

How much?

The amount you are allowed to pay in AVCs/FSAVCs will depend on how much you are already contributing to the main company pension scheme. The overall limit on employee contributions is 15% of earnings. So if you are paying 5% to the main scheme, you can pay another 10% in extra contributions. If you are lucky enough to be a member of a 'non-contributory' scheme, where the employer foots the bill, you could invest the whole 15% yourself in an AVC/FSAVC scheme.

Added scope for making AVCs/FSAVCs may arise if your main scheme contributions are related to your basic pay only but you have received extra income in the form of bonuses, overtime or commission. As contribution limits are set on the whole of your taxable earnings, your extra contributions can take into account any additional income on top of your basic pay up to the usual earnings cap, £87,600 for the 1998/99 tax year. Similarly, where employers have made an allowance for the basic state pension in calculating their own and staff contributions (this is done where a scheme counts the basic state pensions towards the total of two-thirds final salary pension), there is also extra income against which top-up contributions can be made.

How little?

You can make either regular monthly contributions or one-off lump sum payments into AVC/FSAVC schemes. Most people like to put a modest amount aside each month, but lump sum payments can be made if you have received a windfall or prefer to wait until the end of the year to see how much you can afford. You could do both – save something regularly and top up with a lump sum if you have spare cash.

If you decide to make regular contributions, be sure to check that you won't be penalized if you need to stop or reduce your savings.

Minimum contribution limits for each type of saving are set by the AVC/FSAVC providers themselves. Regular monthly contributions can start as low as £10 or £20, but many FSAVC providers set higher minimums. Lump sum contributions typically start at £1,000, but some providers will accept less.

Tax relief

Income tax relief is given on all AVCs/FSAVCs whether they are paid as regular or one-off contributions, thus boosting the amount you save. Though the extra pension you receive at retirement will be liable to tax as income, the fact that your contributions receive tax relief at outset does give them a headstart over other forms of saving.

AVCs versus FSAVCs

AVCs

All occupational pension schemes nowadays must offer additional voluntary contribution facilities to their members. The AVC normally works on a 'money purchase' basis, even where the main scheme is a final salary arrangement. This means the extra pension generated by these contributions will depend on the amount saved, charges deducted, investment performance and annuity rates at the time of retirement.

Some pension schemes provide for AVCs to be invested in the main scheme fund, but the majority invite outside providers, such as life insurance companies and building societies, to run their facilities. It is normally the scheme trustees who decide which companies will do this job. The chief drawback is the restricted choice. Some schemes offer only one type of AVC although others may provide two or three investment choices with different providers. The main advantage of in-house AVCs is that the charges are generally significantly lower than on 'free standing' AVCs. The AVC provider is able to offer a more competitive charging structure because of the economies of scale of dealing with the whole workforce and because the employer is carrying out part of the administration by deducting individual contributions at source and passing them on in bulk.

One possible disadvantage, if you are considering early retirement, is that some AVCs may still penalize those who want to take a pension before the company's normal retirement age. Although current AVC contracts do not, where a pension scheme set up its AVC facility some years ago then an old, less flexible charging structure may still apply.

FSAVCs

FSAVCs were introduced in October 1987. They are now offered by a large number of life insurance companies and by some unit and investment trust managers. Employees can choose from any of these schemes and while their existing pension scheme trustees are informed they are not told exactly how much an employee is saving. Like most in-house AVCs, the free-standing versions work on a money-purchase basis. So the amount of additional pension they produce at retirement will depend on how much you save, the level of charges, investment returns and annuity rates at retirement. The charging structures on FSAVCs are rarely as attractive as those on in-house arrangements. Costs are usually higher, partly because of the extra expense involved in setting up and administering an individual contract but also because commission or some other form of remuneration is often paid to a salesman. Their main advantage is the greater freedom of investment choice which they offer. They enable employees to go direct to the best provider of the type of investment scheme they favour. If they can generate returns superior to an in-house scheme, this can more than offset any extra charges. Investment choices are discussed in more detail below.

An FSAVC will not normally be affected by any change of job, either. Instead of having to stop and start a new arrangement, as you would with an AVC, you can simply continue with your FSAVC when you join a new employer's pension scheme. You may even be able to convert it into a personal pension contract without charge, if you move to an employer with no pension scheme or you become self-employed.

AVC/FSAVC Investment Choices

Before deciding on whether to use an in-house AVC or FSAVC, you will need to examine the investment options offered and consider the alternatives.

Deposit accounts

AVCs are offered by a number of leading banks and building societies. FSAVCs offered by life insurance companies usually provide a cash fund option which works in the same way.

Deposit-based AVCs are like ordinary bank or building society accounts except that interest is paid without tax deducted. The monetary value of your savings does not fluctuate. The growth in the fund occurs solely through the build-up of contributions and the addition of interest credited to your account. As with ordinary savings accounts, the interest payments on these deposits fluctuate in line with general interest rates.

The stability of these schemes makes them attractive to employees within five years of retirement who do not want to take any risks with their pension. However, for young contributors they are not advisable. Conventional wisdom and historical evidence shows that over the longer term share-related investments will provide better returns and give more protection against inflation. Long-term studies show that cash deposits normally tend to produce the worst returns, except over very short periods.

With profits

The most popular in-house AVCs are with profits schemes. With profits FSAVC plans are also available. Offered by traditional, long-established life insurance companies, with profit funds provide savers with access to investment in shares and other real assets without all the risks associated with direct investment in the stock market.

When you invest on a with profits basis your contributions are put into a fund which invests in a mixture of UK and international shares, commercial property, fixed interest securities and cash. Returns on these investments are added to your savings in the form of regular bonuses. The bonus system is designed to smooth out fluctuations in investment markets. When conditions are good, some returns are held in reserve so falls can be cushioned if the market turns down. A final bonus is usually added when benefits are taken, to make up for any growth which has not been passed on.

A good with profits AVC/FSAVC can provide a useful halfway house between a deposit account and an investment linked plan. These schemes will appeal to investors who are within five to ten years of retirement who want a relatively low risk route with some scope for growth.

Unit linked funds

These schemes are also offered by insurance companies. They usually provide a range of specialist investment funds. However, most people tend to prefer a managed fund which holds a spread of UK and international shares, property and fixed interest securities. Although this is a similar investment mix to that found in a with profits fund, the progress of your investment can be very different. The value of a managed fund will fluctuate in line with the market value of the underlying investments. There are no reserves to cushion the fund against market downturns, but, equally, no gains are held back from investors when investment conditions are good.

To get the best out of this type of scheme you really need to be a long-term investor with more than five years to go until you reach pension age. When you get to around five years from retirement, experts often advise gradually switching your savings into a gilt fund to protect it against a sudden downturn in the market. Some schemes carry out these switches automatically.

Unit and investment trusts

Unit and investment trusts have become increasingly popular with savers in recent years and some companies have started offering FSAVC schemes. They are less likely to be found as in-house schemes, but this is not necessarily a disadvantage as their charges tend to be very competitive anyway.

Unit and investment trust managers offer ranges of specialist funds investing mainly in UK and overseas shares. Fund values will fluctuate in line with the underlying share prices and the more specialist the trusts are, the more volatile they are likely to be. This type of scheme will tend to be most suitable for those savers with a reasonably adequate main pension who want to be more adventurous with their AVC contributions and are willing to take a risk to secure a higher return.

Which Type of AVC?

It is not strictly necessary to make an either/or decision. You can invest in AVCs and FSAVCs at the same time if you want to, provided the combined contribution does not exceed the official 15% limit. In practice, however, splitting your contributions may mean you pay higher charges overall. Where there are flat rate charges on either type of scheme, they will have a bigger impact on smaller contributions. However, you might decide to make regular savings via, say, an in-house scheme if you are satisfied that it offers good value and then place lump sum contributions in FSAVCs for added variety.

An in-house AVC scheme is likely to be the best option for most employees because of the lower costs involved, although, there may be good reasons for not using this scheme if it does not meet your needs or the provider has a poor past performance record. For example, if a deposit based scheme is the only choice available and you still have more than five years to go until retirement, you may be better off using an investment linked FSAVC.

If your AVC scheme is investment linked, find out how the provider's past returns compare with competitors. Your pension department should be able to provide you with performance comparisons. Or look at the performance of a company's other products in publications such as *Money Management*, which produce surveys of with profits endowments and unit linked funds. This will give you an indication of its investment skills. Although past performance is no guarantee for the future, particularly for with profits policies, it is an important consideration. Charges should always be considered carefully especially if you are planning an early retirement. Make sure there are no penalties involved if you want to take the benefits before normal pension age.

Taking Your AVC/FSAVC Benefits

AVCs/FSAVCs are treated as part of your company pension arrangement both in terms of contribution limits and the benefits you get from them. This means that even though the amount of pension you can get with your extra savings will depend on the size of the fund you have accumulated and the level of annuity rates at your retirement, it will nevertheless be subject to the overall limit of two-thirds of final salary when combined with your main pension. You will also have to take the benefits from your AVCs/FSAVCs at the same time as you take your main scheme benefits, although the government is proposing to make it possible for them to be taken at different times.

The form in which you can take your AVC benefits will depend on when you began making contributions:

- If you started before 8 April 1987, you will have the choice of taking all or part of them as a tax-free cash lump sum, provided the total amount of cash you take does not exceed the limit, currently one and a half times your final salary or £150,000 whichever is the greater. If you are intending to take some of your pension in cash anyway, then it is usually a good idea to take the AVC benefit in cash where possible, because this will leave you with a larger main scheme pension that can benefit from future increases.
- If you start making AVCs after 8 April 1987, or have made FSAVCs, they must be used to gain extra pension through the purchase of an annuity from an insurance company. The type of annuity you can buy with these contributions may be laid

down by the scheme trustees, although they may be prepared
to take your wishes into account. (For more about pension
options at retirement and annuities see Chapter 11.)

Added Years

Some pension schemes, notably those in the public sector, give
employees the option of buying 'added years' as an alternative to
money purchase AVCs. In this way, employees can get extra pension
which is treated the same as their pension from the main scheme. In
a 'one-sixtieth' scheme, buying another year would give you an
additional slice of pension equal to an extra one-sixtieth of your final
salary: the same amount you would have got if you had worked an
extra year.

Buying added years is usually not cheap – your own pension department will tell you the cost. It will be calculated by the scheme's
actuaries, who will work out how much needs to be invested to produce
the required pension at your expected retirement age taking account
of long-term interest rates. The advantage is that you can look forward
to a guaranteed amount of pension subject to the same increases in
payment as your main pension. In the public sector, this means it will
be fully inflation linked. With an AVC, on the other hand, the end
amount of pension is not guaranteed because it will depend on investment returns and annuity rates.

Too Much Pension?

When AVCs are used to buy 'added years', there is no risk of over-
stepping the Inland Revenue's pension limits because the extra amount
of pension that has been purchased is known in advance. However,
most AVCs operate on a money-purchase basis, which means it is
impossible to know for certain how much extra pension has been
produced until retirement is actually reached. If the pension from the
AVCs then takes the total pension over the limit of two-thirds of
earnings, any overfunding is paid back from the AVC arrangement

as a cash sum. There is an automatic tax deduction of 33% for basic rate taxpayers, with an additional charge for higher rate taxpayers.

Although overfunding could occur if an employee pays high contributions into an AVC and there are good investment returns, most people have so much ground to make up that they rarely get anywhere near breaching the limit. If you suspect there may be a problem, check with your pensions department and AVC provider.

Topping up Your Personal Pension

Salary sacrifice

If you are an employee and you have a personal pension, you may or may not have been successful in persuading your employer to contribute to it also. If you have not, or if you would like to increase your contributions, you could consider making a 'salary sacrifice'. This involves asking your employer to pay part of your salary directly into your pension. The advantage is that your employer will not have to pay National Insurance contributions on this money, and may therefore be prepared to contribute more than you actually sacrifice.

Backdating your contributions

Very few people manage to pay maximum contributions into their pension plan year by year. With personal pensions, unlike company schemes, it is actually possible to go back and take up your unused allowances.

There are two methods of taking up previous years' allowances. One way is to 'carry back' your contribution. In this case you simply ask the Inland Revenue to set off the pension contribution you are paying in this tax year against your earnings last year. You will then obtain tax relief at the rate which would have applied then – particularly advantageous if you were paying a higher rate of tax last year than you are this year. To carry out this procedure you should send to the Tax Inspector the Personal Pension Policy Certificate which you will receive from the pension company when you make your investment, specifying that it is to be set against your previous year's earnings. The Tax Inspector will either give you a refund of tax or set the relief against tax you are due to pay in the future. You can also make up for missed contributions over the past six years. This process is called, rather confusingly, 'carry forward' of contributions. Before you can do this, though, you must pay the maximum contribution in the current tax year, or if you are carrying back as well, the previous tax year. You can then start topping up past years' contributions, beginning with the earliest year. You will need a special form if you are catching up on missed contributions. This should be available from your pension provider.

Bear in mind that although the amount of the missing contributions which you can pay is calculated in relation to past years, tax relief is granted against your tax bill in the tax year in which you are actually paying the contribution. So be sure not to 'over-contribute'. In other words, don't let your contributions exceed your taxable income, because you won't qualify for tax relief on the excess.

It is a good idea to discuss the procedures for carrying back and carrying forward pension contributions with a competent financial adviser to ensure you make the best possible use of these facilities.

Other Ways of Making Tax Efficient Savings for Retirement

Many people are understandably reluctant to lock away all their savings in a pension, even though they know they must put aside more money for their retirement. Although other products do not give the same up-front tax relief you get with a pension, there are a variety of tax efficient savings and investment plans which can be used for building up retirement funds. Your choice will depend on how close to retirement you are and how much risk you want to take.

- **Tax Exempt Special Savings Accounts (TESSAs).** A low-risk option if you have around five years to retirement. Tessas are tax-free accounts offered by bank and building societies. Returns tend to be more competitive than ordinary deposit accounts for the amounts invested. Interest on the accounts is tax free, provided your capital is left untouched for five years. Rates are mainly variable, but some fixed interest deals may be on offer. Minimum investment starts at £1, but some accounts require sums of £100 or more. A maximum of £9,000 can be invested in a Tessa – £3,000 in the first year and up to £1,800 in the following years. (Tessas taken out before the introduction of individual savings accounts (ISAs) in April 1999 will be allowed to run their course.)

- **National Savings.** It is never a bad idea to include some Index Linked Savings Certificates among your investments as a hedge against a resurgence in inflation. This way you know you are guaranteed to match rising prices and get a bonus on top. The 12th Issue is offering inflation linking plus 2.5% per annum over five years. Returns are tax free. Between £100 and £10,000 can be invested. Fixed rate National Savings Certificates are also worth considering if the rates are competitive.

- **Personal Equity Plans (PEPs).** If you have five years or more to go to retirement, an investment in shares is likely to provide better returns than a deposit account. The cheapest and easiest way to buy shares is through a unit or investment trust PEP. Up to £6,000 per tax year can be invested. Any income or capital gains which PEPs generate will be tax free. In April 1999 PEPs will be replaced by ISAs, but existing PEP holdings can be left invested until required.

- **Corporate bond PEPs.** Not all PEPs invest in shares; this variety invest in fixed interest securities issued by public companies. They are less volatile than shares and are worth considering if you are reasonably close to retirement, do not mind some risk and want an investment which will pay a high income after you stop work. Yields averaged 6.4% in the first quarter of 1998. If interest rates fall, the capital value of these PEPs will be given a boost.

- **Individual Savings Accounts (ISAs).** To be introduced by the Government in April 1999 to replace TESSAs and PEPs.

They will undoubtedly become an important element in most people's retirement planning. In the first year £7,000 can be invested, after that the limit will be £5,000, of which up to £1,000 can be in life insurance premiums and £1,000 (£3,000 in year 1) in a deposit account. The remainder, or if investors prefer the whole ISA, can be invested in shares direct or through unit or investment trusts. All the growth and interest in an ISA will be tax free.

- **Zero dividend preference shares.** Zeros are one type of share issued by split capital investment trusts. They pay no income but provide a reasonably secure, predetermined rate of capital growth. The returns they offer are comparable to but slightly better than those available on government securities. Investors will have no tax to pay on this growth, provided it falls within their annual capital gains tax allowance currently of £6,800. Zeros can be purchased directly from investment trust managers or through a stockbroker.

- **Roll-up funds.** These are off-shore funds, similar to unit trusts, domiciled in countries with low tax regimes such as the Channel Islands. Their attraction is that investment returns can be accumulated or 'rolled-up' tax free in the funds until they are sold. They are then taxed at your current income tax rate, so they are particularly suitable if you expect to pay a lower rate of tax after retirement. If you retire abroad, you may even be able to avoid tax altogether. They are offered by many UK fund managers.

7 ‖ Pensions for Directors

Senior executives and directors of companies who want to boost their retirement provision have a number of extra pension choices in addition to ordinary company schemes or personal pension plans.

One of the traditional options for directors has been an executive pension plan. Directors who run their own businesses, on the other hand, may wish to consider setting up their pension plans in the form of a 'small self-administered pension scheme' which they can call on for business finance if necessary. For high earning employees whose ordinary pension arrangements have reached the limit imposed by the earnings 'cap', an 'unapproved' pension scheme may be of interest.

Executive Pension Plans

Although executive pension arrangements are classified as company pension schemes, they are usually set up on an individual basis. In the past there were multi-member schemes, but extra regulation imposed on group schemes by the Pensions Act which came into force in 1997 made such arrangements less popular.

The main advantage of executive pension schemes over personal pensions is the greater flexibility in the contribution limits and benefit levels. Where executives have neglected their pension provision in the past, these schemes can be used to provide a larger pension in a shorter time.

Executive plans can be particularly suitable for small businesses for the following reasons:

- They are a more tax efficient way of moving money from the company to the directors than, for example, paying higher salaries or extra dividends.
- The directors can decide, within certain limits, the level and timing of the contributions.
- Contributions are allowable as a business expense and can be offset against corporation tax for companies, or income tax for partnerships and sole proprietors.
- Funds are protected from creditors in the event of a business failure as policies are written in trust.
- Death benefits paid on a discretionary basis can help a business cover the cost of meeting an inheritance tax liability should a director die before retirement.
- Loan facilities may also be available. (For details of the conditions attached to these loans, see the section on small self-administered schemes, page 98.)

Investment

Like personal pension plans, executive pensions operate on a 'money purchase' basis. Thus, the size of your pension fund at retirement and hence the amount of your pension depends largely on the growth of the contributions invested.

Most plans are offered by insurance companies and the investment choices are similar to those of personal pension plans. The main options are with profits, unit linked and unit trust funds. These funds are discussed in more detail in Chapter 6. For greater freedom of investment choice, including buying shares in your own business, you could consider a fully or hybrid self-administered scheme.

Benefits and contributions

The benefit limits for executive pension plans are:

- **A pension** of up to two-thirds of final salary which can be taken on retirement, normally between age 60 and 75.
- **A tax-free lump sum** of up to one and a half times final salary

is available at retirement (it may be possible to take the entire executive pension fund as tax-free cash because this is calculated as a proportion of the final salary and not as a proportion of the fund).

- **Death benefits** of up to four times salary, plus a return of employee's contributions with interest, can be paid as a lump sum if the holder dies before retirement.
- **A spouse's or dependant's pension** of up to two-thirds of the holder's pension can be provided on death before or after retirement.

Contribution limits are:

Employees do not have to pay anything, but if they do their contributions must not exceed 15% of their earnings. Employers must contribute something in order for the scheme to qualify as a tax-deductible pension arrangement, but their maximum contributions are not fixed. They are based on a maximum benefit calculation linked to the employee's length of service with the employer. The important point to note is that benefits are related to length of service rather than membership of the pension scheme, so the company can pay extra large contributions into the scheme to make up for years of service when no pension provision was made. Contributions can therefore be as large as 100% of salary, although over a working life they are more likely to average around 20%.

The maximum benefits which contributions can fund vary according to when a plan was started:

- **For plans taken out before March 1987.** A pension of two-thirds of final salary can be achieved after ten years as long as the holder is aged 60 or over.
- **For plans taken out between March 1987 and March 1989.** The maximum pension is one-thirtieth of final salary multiplied by the number of years of service. Therefore the overall maximum of two-thirds (20/30ths) of final salary is available after a minimum of 20 years' service.
- **For plans taken out after March 1989.** Maximum benefits

are as for plans taken out after March 1987 except that the earnings cap applies to final salary calculations (for 1998/99 it was set at £87,600; it is increased annually in line with the retail price index).

Final salary:

With executive pension plans, the definition of final salary can be either:

- **The highest earnings** in any one of the five years preceding retirement, or
- **The yearly average earnings** over three or more consecutive years ending not earlier than 10 years before retirement.

The second definition must be used for controlling directors (those owning 20% or more of a company). This is to stop directors paying themselves a very high salary in just one year shortly before they retire in order to boost their pensions.

Overfunding

If large contributions are made to an executive pension scheme and investment performance is good, by the time a director reaches retirement the benefits that can be bought with the fund may exceed Inland Revenue limits. There may be ways round the problem, such as buying additional spouse's pension. Otherwise the excess amount will have to be paid back to the employer, less 40% tax, or where it arises from the employee's contributions paid back to the employee less a tax charge of 33% for basic rate taxpayers and 48% for higher rate taxpayers.

Small Self-Administered Schemes

For controlling directors and executives of small businesses who are reluctant to tie up too much of their resources in a pension plan for fear that they may need the money for the business itself, a variation of executive pension plans which could prove useful is a small self-administered scheme (SSAS).

Besides giving directors more say in how their funds are invested (though this facility is also available nowadays under a self invested personal pension (SIPP)), the funds built up in a SSAS can be used to provide loans to the company and to purchase new business premises. However, these attractions must be balanced against the extra complexity involved in this type of pension scheme. A trust deed will be necessary to establish it and all the directors who are being provided with pensions will usually be appointed as trustees. They are responsible for running the scheme and can determine the investment policy of the fund, although they will normally appoint professionals to carry out most of the work and to guide them through Inland Revenue and Social Security regulations. Many insurance companies, consultants and other professional advisers offer service packages to cover the actuarial, legal and administration requirements of SSASs. An investment manager may also be employed. One of the Inland Revenue rules requires that there is an independent trustee, known as a 'pensioneer trustee', to ensure that the scheme is run correctly and is not wound up improperly. People acting as pensioneer trustees have to be approved by the Inland Revenue. Someone to fill this role will usually be provided by the company administering the scheme or the directors' professional advisers.

The contribution and benefit levels for SSASs are the same as for executive pension plans. Directors with their own business may especially appreciate the flexibility that such a scheme offers to vary company contributions each year, within certain limits, in line with changes in profits. High contributions can be made when profits are good to offset potential corporation tax bills.

It is normally recommended that the employer pays for the full costs of the scheme. This is not only because they are tax deductible but, since no National Insurance contributions have to be made on the contributions, they also help reduce the company's National Insurance bill.

SSAS investment

The directors, who are the trustees, can appoint a manager to run the scheme's investment portfolio or they can decide their own investment strategy and run it themselves. They can include a substantial investment in their own company. However, they are not permitted to make any investments which might result in a personal benefit to the members of the scheme. They cannot, for example, buy shares in the parent company from members of the scheme or their families or associated companies. When deciding on the investment strategy, due consideration must also be given to the need to have the funds available to provide pensions for members when they reach retirement.

The Inland Revenue must be informed within 90 days of the purchase or sale of any investments in property and unquoted shares. Loans to or from connected companies must also be reported. Failure to abide by such rules can result in the loss of Inland Revenue approval for the scheme.

- **Permitted investments.** Investments can include quoted stocks and shares, pooled funds such as unit and investment trusts, unit linked funds, commercial property, mortgages and loans, foreign currency, traded options, cash funds and deposit accounts. Investment in residential property is not normally permitted.
- **Own shares.** The pension fund can acquire shares in the parent company as long as the total value of the shares together with any loans to the company never exceeds 50% of the fund or 25% of the contributions to a scheme during the first two years. The price of the shares must be determined independently. Also, any shares purchased must not represent more than 30% of the voting power of the company.
- **Loans.** Both individual executive pension schemes and SSASs can be used to provide business loans under certain conditions. Among the stipulations is that the loans must be for genuine commercial reasons, such as the purchase of capital items for use in the business or the extension or modernization of working

accommodation. Others rules are that the business must pay a commercial rate of interest on the loan, and the amount of the loan, plus the value of any shares held by the scheme, must not exceed 25% of the value of the pension arrangement in the first two years, and 50% thereafter. In the case of individual schemes, the loan must be repaid by the time the executive reaches normal pension age.

- **Property.** Many small businesses have set up SSASs for the sole purpose of buying property for company use. The property becomes an asset of the pension fund and must be leased back to the company at a commercial rent. An independent valuer must be employed to assess the rent and carry out periodic reviews. The company itself will get corporation tax relief on the rent it pays to the pension fund, while the fund can reclaim the tax from the Inland Revenue.

However, a major property purchase may not normally be permitted by the Inland Revenue if the directors are within, say, 10 years of retirement because of the need to have sufficient liquid funds available to finance future pensions.

The cost of an SSAS

The charges made by providers of SSASs vary considerably. A major factor will be the range of services included in the package. Charges may take the form of a percentage of the contributions, but a flat fee structure is more usual, consisting of a basic sum for the scheme plus a further fee for each member. If the trustees employ an investment manager to run the fund, this will normally cost extra. As a scheme should always be set up with the help of professional advisers, they should be able to recommend the most cost-effective approach.

Hybrid SSASs

A cheaper option for smaller businesses or directors who are interested in limited self-investment only is a hybrid SSAS. These arrangements are a halfway house between a straightforward executive pension scheme and a fully self-administered scheme. Offered by insurance companies, the hybrid versions require that a substantial annual contribution, say £5,000 per annum, is invested in the funds managed by the insurer, while the remainder can be self-invested by the trustees. Subject to the minimum required by the provider, the exact split will be at the discretion of the directors.

Hybrid SSASs are generally regarded as the most cost-effective option for businesses contributing less than around £12,000 per annum. Charges are typically on a percentage basis. However, for larger investments the flat rate fee structures of fully self-administered schemes are likely to be more advantageous.

Retirement options

At retirement, the proceeds of an executive pension plan (including SSAS) can be used to buy an annuity to provide a regular pension immediately, or the annuity purchase can be delayed and income drawdown or phased retirement chosen instead (for more details of the various choices available see Chapter 11). One of the snags of an executive pension plan is that because it is classified as a company scheme the type of annuity which must be purchased with any benefits built up since April 1997 is laid down by the Pensions Act. It must be a joint life annuity which provides a pension rising in line with the retail price index or 5%, whichever is lower.

Unapproved Pension Schemes

Although executive pension schemes may allow companies to provide directors and executives with above average pensions, there are limits on the benefits. Since 1989 the Government has imposed an 'earnings cap', that is, a ceiling on the amount of salary that can be taken into account when calculating pension contributions and benefits.

The earnings cap has affected all members of company pension schemes which were set up after the 1989 Budget and anyone who joined an existing company pension scheme after 1 June 1989. It is set at £87,600 for the 1998/99 tax year, and is normally increased in line with the retail price index each year. Since price inflation is usually less than wage inflation, therefore, the relative value of the cap is gradually being eroded.

However, this does not actually prevent employers from providing extra pensions. The Inland Revenue allows employers to set up 'unapproved' retirement benefit schemes. These are recognized as genuine pension arrangements, but are not granted the tax concessions which approved schemes receive: hence the term 'unapproved'. They can be either funded or unfunded schemes.

Funded schemes

Under a 'funded unapproved retirement benefit' (furb) scheme, the employer pays contributions into a fund to provide a pension relating to an employee's earnings in excess of the cap on an approved scheme. The fund is written in trust for the employee. Furbs are normally money purchase arrangements, which means the size of the fund at retirement and the benefits it produces will depend mainly on contributions and investment growth. These benefits can be added to those payable under the company's main pension scheme. There is no formal limit on either the contributions or the amount of pension which can be provided under furbs.

Unlike an ordinary money purchase pension scheme, however, the fund will be subject to income and capital gains tax of 20% and 34% respectively. Still, these are lower rates than higher rate tax payers would have to pay on ordinary taxed savings accounts. The contributions themselves are treated for tax purposes as benefits in kind, so he or she will have to pay income tax on them. However, for the employer they are expenses and can be claimed against corporation tax, so some employers are prepared to foot the employee's income tax liability as well. Since April 1998, employers have had to pay National Insurance on the pension contributions.

At retirement the fund can be used to buy an annuity to provide a pension which will be taxed in the normal way. The most popular option, however, is to take the whole fund as a tax-free lump sum. In the event of death before retirement, a return of fund can be paid out under a discretionary trust so that it is free of inheritance tax.

Unfunded schemes

A less common arrangement is an unfunded unapproved retirement benefit scheme. As the terminology suggests, the employer pays no contributions into such a scheme and no specific fund is built up. Instead, the pension benefits are paid out of company funds when the employee retires. At this point the employer can also claim an allowance against corporation tax.

One advantage of this arrangement is that the employee has no tax to pay until the benefits are received: all lump sums and pensions are then subject to tax. However, any death benefits, if they are paid under a discretionary trust, should escape inheritance tax.

The main drawback of this type of scheme is the apparent lack of security. Because there is no fund which is legally separate from the company's assets and in trust for the employee, there is the risk that in the event of the company being taken over or going into liquidation an employee's benefits may suffer. Employees should take professional advice before agreeing to this type of scheme.

8 || *Employment Breaks and Time Spent Working Abroad – how they Affect Your Pension*

Nowadays an unbroken working life is becoming increasingly rare. A flexible labour market means that an increasing number of people are experiencing at least one period of unemployment during their career. Many companies take staff on short-term contracts so they can cut back quickly if demand falls. You may even choose to drop out of the UK labour market for a while. Many women, for example, take career breaks to bring up a young family or help look after elderly relatives. Or you may decide to retrain or spend a period travelling or working overseas.

One of the snags with having breaks in your working life is that they can damage your pension prospects. Stopping your pension contributions even for a limited time will reduce your future retirement income. If you spend a period not working, therefore, it is important to look carefully at how it has affected your pension and what, if anything, you can do to make up for any setbacks.

Planning Ahead

If possible, plan ahead. Although periods of unemployment are unpredictable and can last anything from a few weeks to several years, the possibility that you may suffer a period out of work in the future increases the need to start building your pension as fast as you can as early as you can. So if you are offered membership of an employer's pension scheme, it is usually advisable to accept without delay.

Alternatively, start or increase contributions to your own personal pension plan. Be careful when selecting a plan to ensure that it can accommodate stops and starts in contributions or possibly the complete cessation of contributions without penalty. (See Chapter 4 for more details on choosing a personal pension.) If you know your job is temporary it may be better to make single premium contributions so there is no likelihood of heavy up-front deductions to cover commission payments. For women, it is particularly important to save as much as possible during the early working years, as this is often the time when they have the most spare income available. When they return to work after a career break, many women take part-time jobs until their children are older which limits the amount they can put into their pension. The impact of the break on their pension is usually significant. The average mother starts a career break aged 26 and remains at home for some six-and-a-half years. Calculations by an insurance company show that a woman taking such a break would see her pension fund drop by nearly 40%.

During the Break

Find out what happens to each element of your pension while you are not working. Even if there is little that you can do to boost it, you will be better prepared when you start working again.

- **Your state pension.** Try to make sure your National Insurance record is maintained when you are not working, otherwise you could end up with a reduced basic state pension at retirement. National Insurance credits are normally given to anyone registering as unemployed and claiming Jobseekers Allowance (the name now given to unemployment benefit) during the first 26 weeks of unemployment. After that period, Jobseekers Allowance is means tested. If you do not qualify for the allowance, you can still receive NI credits provided you continue to register as unemployed. The only people who do not need to register in this situation are men aged over 60 who receive automatic credits, provided they do not leave the country for more than six months in the year.

If you are on a Government approved training course you will also receive credits. However, if you follow any other sort of training course or return to higher education, no credits are given. People who stay at home to look after young children or dependent relatives should qualify for Home Responsibilities Protection (HRP). This effectively reduces the number of qualifying years you would otherwise need for a full pension. HRP is given automatically to the main person in receipt of child benefit for a child under age 16, or to someone receiving income support to look after a sick or disabled person at home. But you will need to apply for it if you are looking after someone who is getting attendance allowance or a similar benefit.

National Insurance credits only count towards the basic state pension, not towards the state earnings related scheme (SERPS).

- **Your company pension.** Once you stop working, your membership of a company pension scheme will automatically come to an end. You have various options regarding the benefits you have built up in the scheme: you can leave them where they are and they will be revalued in line with the retail price index up to a maximum of 5% per year until you reach retirement; you can transfer them straightaway to your own personal pension plan or similar insurance plan; or you can wait until you are working again and move them into your next employer's scheme. (These options are discussed in greater detail in Chapter 3.) It is normally wise to wait until you start working again before making a final decision.

If you have been a member for less than two years, you may be given no choice but to take a refund of your pension contributions less a tax charge of 20%. The best thing you can do with that money is to invest it immediately as a lump sum contribution in a personal pension to cover your period of employment which will be treated as non-pensionable. It is unlikely that this sum will be equivalent to the maximum you could have invested during that period in a personal pension, so if you have extra cash available, you can top it up and receive full tax relief.

- **Your personal pension.** In theory, if you have a personal pension you will have to cease contributions when you stop working because under current rules you are only allowed to make pension contributions out of earned income. In practice, however, assuming you have not paid the maximum permitted pension contributions in previous years, you may be able to go on contributing to your plan for up to two years and still receive tax relief. This is because there is a provision which allows you to pay a contribution and have it treated by the Inland Revenue as having been paid in the previous tax year. Your pension provider should be able to supply the forms you will need. More details about carrying back contributions are given in Chapter 6.

  If your career break is likely to be a lengthy one, and you previously had a regular savings plan, you should find out how the pension company's charging structure will affect the value of your plan. It may be more cost-effective to switch the transfer value to a single premium plan. It is a good idea in this situation to seek professional advice about your best course of action.

- **Other savings.** Although you are not allowed to contribute to a pension policy during your time off work, it is worth considering other forms of saving if you have spare cash available. The most tax efficient options are discussed in more detail in Chapter 6.

When You Return to Work

You will need to carry out a thorough reassessment of your pension position when you return to work and look at ways in which you can make up for the period of missed contributions. Much will depend on whether or not your new employer provides a pension scheme and what type of scheme it is.

- **Your state pension.** Although you should have been receiving NI credits if you were entitled to them, the DSS has been known to make mistakes. To make sure you have been correctly credited, you should request a free state pension forecast from the Department of Social Security on your return to work. Ask your local DSS for a request form BR19. If you did not receive credits because, say, you went back to college or were travelling abroad, you could consider paying voluntary NI contributions. You have up to six years to make up for gaps in your NI record.
- **A company pension scheme.** It usually makes sense to rejoin a scheme as soon as you can. Where the scheme is final salary related, the more years' service you clock up the better; and in a money purchase scheme the sooner you restart the more you will benefit from the build-up of your employer's contributions as well as your own. In a money purchase scheme, your employer may offer a 'contribution matching' arrangement offering a choice of contribution levels to employees which the company will match. If you can afford to, start with maximum contributions to make up for lost time. With either type of scheme you should consider making additional voluntary contributions (AVCs) to boost your final benefits. Remember it is possible to make lump sum payments to these schemes if you have accumulated some savings. If you are employed in the public sector it is also worthwhile finding out if you can buy added years. (See Chapter 6 for more details.)

  If you were previously a member of another company pension scheme, you should consider taking a transfer value from that scheme and using it to buy benefits in your new scheme. This may be attractive if you expect to remain with your new employer until retirement, but you will definitely need to take professional advice before making a decision. (See Chapter 3 for more details.)

- **A personal pension.** Your new employer may offer you membership of a group personal pension plan. With this type of arrangement, individual plans are set up with a company of the employer's choice. The advantages are that charges may be lower because of the economies of scale and the employer will usually make a contribution to the scheme.

  If you already had a personal pension before you stopped working which still offers good terms, you could ask your employer to make contributions to that one instead. If that is not possible you could contribute to both. There is no restriction on the number of personal plans you can have as long as your total savings do not exceed the contributions limits. If your new employer offers no pension arrangement, you will definitely need to start contributing to your own personal pension plan. Before restarting an existing plan, check whether it is still competitive before you re-start your contributions. Another provider may offer a better deal.

  Remember, when you do start contributing again you will need to save more than before if you want to end up with the same level of pension fund that you had originally expected. A woman who has taken the typical career break would have to almost double the payments to her pension plan in order to have the same pension she would have had if she hadn't taken the break! If you can't afford so much, because you have a lower income or are working part-time, pay in what you can manage. It is certainly better to save something than not save at all. You should aim to increase your contributions in future if you get a pay rise or you return to full-time work.

Working Abroad

If you have spent time working abroad, you may have a gap in your UK pension record. To add to the complexity, you may have acquired pension benefits while you were abroad.

- **State pension.** In general, when you go to work in another country, you will have to make social security contributions to the local state insurance scheme. If you work abroad for a UK employer, you will normally remain within the UK National Insurance regime for the first year.

A potential snag of becoming insured in another country is that not all countries have the same minimum qualifying periods for building up a state pension, nor do they pay their retirement pensions at the same ages. Fortunately, there is a multilateral agreement within the European Union that the insurance record you have in one member country counts towards the minimum period of qualification in another. Be sure to keep a record of your local social security number together with any other relevant documentation covering the period you worked abroad for when you make your claim. When you reach retirement you can claim a pension directly from any EU country that you have been insured in, or you can claim from the EU country you live in when you are getting near pension age and it will pass details of your claim to any other EU country where you have been insured. Each country works out how much pension you are entitled to from what you have paid into its own social security system. It then adds together your insurance in all countries to see if this improves your pension position under its own scheme. Each country decides how it will pay your pension. If you live in another country and are eligible for a UK pension, for example, it can be sent to you every 4 or 13 weeks or paid into your overseas UK bank account.

If you work in other parts of the world, your local contributions may count towards a UK pension when you make a claim or vice versa. Britain has bilateral reciprocal agreements with a number of other countries, such as Cyprus and Jamaica. However, when you go abroad it is important to check the exact position applying to that country. If you want to be sure of not losing any entitlement to a UK pension, it is worth considering paying voluntary UK National Insurance contributions while you are away. You have up to six years to pay contributions after the end of each tax year.

For more information about your social security position when you are abroad, see DSS leaflets NI38 'Social security abroad' and SA29 'Your social security insurance, benefits and health care rights in the European Community'. Other leaflets are also available covering countries with which Britain has reciprocal agreements.

- **Company pension.** If you go abroad to work for a UK company, you can generally join or remain a member of your employer's UK pension scheme while you are away. Your membership can be maintained for up to ten years. The Inland Revenue would normally require you leave the scheme after that, but your employer may be able to negotiate an extension.

One potential problem with being in a UK scheme is that you may be taxed abroad on the contributions your employer makes to your pension if they are considered part of your income. For this reason, your employer may not make specific payments into the scheme on your behalf while you are away but will guarantee to provide you with a pension for that period anyway. The Inland Revenue will allow your overseas service to be taken into account when your final benefits are calculated, provided they do not exceed the usual limits. If you enter into this type of arrangement, be sure to find out how your pension benefits will be affected if the company goes bust or if you decide to leave your job before retirement or even while you are abroad.

If you work for a foreign employer while you are away, you may be expected to join that company's pension scheme if there is one. This could be advantageous if the employer makes contributions, and there may be tax reliefs on your own savings. However, you may have to remain with the company for a minimum period to qualify for a pension and if you leave before retirement there may be a problem transferring the benefits. In such circumstances, if you have a choice, it may be better to ask to remain outside the scheme and make your own savings.

- **Personal pensions and other savings.** You cannot contribute to a personal pension when you work abroad. This is only possible if you have UK earnings. However, you could put part of your pay into a savings scheme in one of the 'offshore' investment centres, such as the Channel Islands, Dublin, the Isle of Man or Luxembourg. The special status of these centres means that little or no tax will be deducted from your savings as they build up.

Ideally you should consult a specialist independent financial adviser for expatriates who can recommend suitable products. Many well-known UK insurers, banks and unit trust companies have offshore subsidiaries with schemes specifically designed for British expatriates. Some products are called pension plans, even though they are not the same as the pension policies you would buy in the UK, and other types of savings schemes in ordinary unit trusts may give you more flexibility. As with any savings contract, it is important to check out the charges (they can be higher on offshore products than in the UK) and the investment performance of the provider. It is better not to commit yourself to a long-term contract which penalizes you if you have to cease paying into the plan.

If you return to the UK, you can stop saving and leave your money offshore to grow in a tax-free environment until you retire and then decide what to do with it. An advantage of this arrangement is that unlike an ordinary on-shore pension plan, you will not be forced to buy an annuity with your offshore savings.

9 || *Early and Late Retirement*

Many working people would like to escape the rat race and retire early. If this is your goal, you must start planning well in advance in order to build up an adequate pension in time. However, you may not be given an option. In recent years, many people have had early retirement forced upon them by employers cutting back on staff. The good thing about this situation is that an employer will often ensure that staff receive a better pension than they would if they were retiring early on their own account.

Not everyone wants to retire early, however. Some people may simply prefer to reduce their working week and retire gradually. If you have a personal pension you can start drawing the income and still continue to work. With an employer's scheme you generally have to stop work altogether before you can take a pension, although the Government is planning to introduce greater flexibility here too. Finally, there are some people who do not want to stop at all and would prefer to continue working after ordinary retirement age.

The way early and late retirement affects your pension varies with different types of schemes:

Early Retirement

The state pension

No provision is made for those who wish to retire early. In fact there is a risk that your state pension could be reduced if you retire before 60 and too large a gap opens up in your National Insurance record. You will get NI credits if you register as unemployed or are eligible for certain benefits, such as sickness benefit. Otherwise it may be worthwhile to consider paying Class 3 voluntary National Insurance contributions. (See DSS leaflet CA08 'National Insurance voluntary contributions'.)

Check your state pension entitlement first by asking for a forecast on form BR19, available from local DSS offices. The only concession is made for men, in that if they retire early they will be credited automatically with National Insurance contributions from the year in which they reach 60 without having to register as unemployed, provided they do not spend more than six months of the year outside the UK. From 6 April 2010 this arrangement will extend to women aged 60.

Even if you are considered to be of normal retirement age by your employer, you cannot claim the state pension until you reach ordinary state retirement age, currently 60 for women and 65 for men. Women claiming a spouse's pension based on their husband's contributions must wait until he is 65. From 2020, women will have to wait until they reach age 65 for their state pension. The retirement age for women will be increased gradually between 2010 and 2020 (see Introduction for more details).

Employer pensions
Retirement ages for men in company schemes have been going down in recent years. Annual surveys by the National Association of Pension Funds, which covers most employers' schemes, show that in 1988 some 69% of all schemes had a normal pensionable age of 65 for men. By 1996 the proportion had dropped to around 60%. Meanwhile the number of schemes setting 60 as the normal retirement age has risen from 19% to over a quarter, with the remainder setting the age somewhere in between. However, companies' normal retirement ages for women have risen. In the past women were usually allowed to retire earlier than men, but schemes must now have the same retirement ages for both sexes which has meant that in most cases the age for women has been brought in line with that for men.

The effect of retiring from a company scheme before the normal pensionable age will depend on the type of scheme to which you belong and the circumstances of your retirement. Whichever type it is, if you are hoping to retire early you should consider making additional voluntary contributions (AVCs) well in advance to build up your pension fund.

- **Final salary schemes.** One of the factors determining the size of the pension you get from this type of scheme is normally the number of years' service you have completed. You will get a fraction of your salary, say one-sixtieth, for each year. If you retire ten years early, for example, you would get ten-sixtieths less than if you waited until normal pensionable age. Many schemes will impose no further reduction if you take voluntary early retirement within, say, two to five years of the normal retirement age, especially if that is 65. Otherwise an early retirement discount factor may be applied to your normal pension entitlement to take account of the longer than expected period for which the pension will have to be paid. A typical reduction in pension is between 3% and 6% for every year that retirement precedes the agreed age. In such cases, retiring five years early could result in a reduction in your pension of between 15% and 30%.

Table 15: Effect of early retirement in final salary pension schemes

How early retirement could affect a pension depending on length of membership, assuming normal retirement is age 65, pension is 1/60th of final salary for each year of service, salary at retirement is £30,000 and there is no early retirement reduction if retirement is within five years of the normal age but 4% per year if earlier.

Retirement age	Years in scheme	Pension entitlement p.a.	Early retirement reduction	Reduced pension p.a.
Member since age 25				
65	40	£20,000	–	–
60	35	£17,500	–	–
55	30	£15,000	20%	£12,000
50	25	£12,500	40%	£7,500
Member since age 45				
65	20	£10,000	–	–
60	15	£7,500	–	£7,500
55	10	£5,000	20%	£4,000
50	5	£2,500	40%	£1,500

If the maximum discount applies, taking voluntary early retirement more than a couple of years ahead of time can lead to a significant loss of pension, especially if you have not been a member of the scheme for very long. Fortunately, maximum discounts are not always applied. You may even be given an enhancement crediting you with the full number of years you would otherwise have worked up to normal retirement date.

A discount-free early retirement may be allowed if:

- You have completed a certain length of service or are within a certain number of years of retirement.
- Your employer is seeking to shed staff and offers early retirement to encourage volunteers.
- You are suffering ill-health and the pension scheme believes your life expectancy has been reduced.

However, even if you are not penalized, your company pension may still fall short of your needs if you were not a member of the scheme for very long. One way round this problem is to ask your employer if it is possible to have a temporary pension boost until you become eligible for the state pension. Some employers will provide 'bridging pensions' for this purpose, which are equivalent to the state pension. Alternatively, an employee may be able to achieve a similar effect by sacrificing part of his future pension in return for an extra pension up to state retirement age. This is known as the 'levelling' option.

- **Money purchase schemes.** No specific level of pension is promised under this type of scheme. The amount paid out will depend on the size of fund that has been built up through contributions and investment growth. The earlier you retire the smaller your fund is likely to be, because you and your employer will have made fewer contributions and those made will have had less time to grow. Retiring five years early may mean your pension fund is around 40% less than it would have been at the normal retirement age. However, your employer might choose to boost your fund to make early retirement a more attractive option if the company is anxious to cut back on staff.

To provide you with a retirement income your pension fund will normally be used to buy an annuity. Annuity rates are lower at younger ages, so this will also reduce the amount of pension you get. Try to make sure the trustees have shopped around for the most competitive annuity rates. If you are retiring early due to ill-health they may be able to get an even better deal for you with an impaired life annuity. If your fund is large enough, you could consider delaying your annuity purchase and opting for income drawdown instead. (See Chapter 11 for more detail about your retirement options.)

Personal pensions

A pension can be drawn from a personal pension from age 50 under Inland Revenue rules. If you have an old-style retirement annuity contract which only allowed retirement from age 60, you can switch it into a personal pension if you wish to take benefits earlier. Those working in certain professions, such as sportsmen and women, are allowed to start taking a pension even younger. For most people, however, taking a pension as early as 50 is likely to prove impractical simply because they have not accumulated a large enough pension fund to provide them with the amount of retirement income they need.

Table 16: The effect of early retirement on a personal pension

Examples of the reductions in fund and pension available at younger ages, based on plan started at age 30 with gross savings of £100 per month, assuming growth rate of 9% p.a. less charges

	Retirement age			
	50	55	60	65
Fund	£57,000	£93,700	£147,000	£228,000
Pension p.a.	£4,900	£8,570	£14,700	£25,400

Source: Legal & General Direct

Fortunately, there is considerable scope for topping up a personal pension if you have not contributed the maximum in the past. You can make up for missed contributions over a six- or even seven-year period through the 'carry back' and 'carry forward' provisions which are explained in Chapter 6. These contributions can be paid in a lump sum.

However, a further snag with early retirement under a personal pension is that, as with money purchase company schemes, the amount of pension your fund will buy will be affected by the fact that annuity rates are lower at younger ages. For this reason, if your pension fund is large enough, it may be worth considering 'income drawdown' instead or 'phased retirement' if you retire early so that you can defer the purchase of the annuity. (See Chapter 11 for more details of your retirement options.)

Another point to bear in mind if you are considering early retirement is whether your pension company will impose a penalty if you start drawing a pension earlier than you originally stated. The charging structure of the pension plan and the commission paid to the salesman may have been based on the term of the contract. If you retire early, the extra charges are taken out then. On policies sold recently this practice is less widespread, but it's always worth checking to be on the safe side.

Late Retirement

The state pension

If you wish to continue working after state retirement age, you can defer taking your state pension for up to five years under the present rules. If you start taking it but then resume working, you can give it up until age 70 if you are a man or 65 if you are a woman. By deferring or giving it up temporarily in this way you can earn extra pension. For more information see DSS leaflet NI192 'Giving up your retirement pension to earn extra'. If you defer by more than seven weeks you will start to earn 'increments' on each element of your pension – basic, graduated and SERPS. The current rate of increment is 7.5% per year.

You can only give up your pension once and you must be ordinarily resident in Great Britain. You cannot backdate your decision to give up your pension. Also, a married man whose wife has a pension based on his NI contributions cannot give up his pension without her consent. This provision will also apply to married women from 6 April 2010, when men will be able to get a basic pension based on their wives' contribution record. From 6 April 2010 you will also be able to put off receiving your pension indefinitely, and it will then be increased by 10.4% a year.

An alternative approach is to take your pension and invest it in your own personal pension or savings account.

If you work beyond state pension age, whether or not you take a pension, you do not have to pay any more NI contributions. If you are not sent a Certificate of Age Exemption automatically by the DSS, you should ask for one to give to your employer so that they know it is no longer necessary to deduct employee NI contributions from your salary. Employer contributions, on the other hand, will have to be continued. If you are self-employed you can also stop paying NI contributions if you work beyond state pension age.

Company pensions

Working beyond the normal retirement date of your pension scheme does not usually cause any problems. But the arrangements will differ between employers and types of schemes.

● **Final salary schemes.** Some employers who want to retain your services may still prefer you to retire at the normal pension age and start drawing your pension, but immediately re-hire you in a non-pensionable capacity. You would then be eligible to take out a personal pension on the basis of your non-pensionable earnings.

   The more usual approach, however, is for you to simply continue working and building up a larger pension in the company scheme. This may be done in one of two ways:
   1 The pension you would have received at your normal retirement age is increased by a given percentage each month.

2 You continue to contribute to the scheme and build up extra years of service. When you eventually retire, your pension is calculated on the usual basis of years of service and earnings at retirement. This approach is beneficial if your previous service with the company was limited. However, there are two potential problems. If you were close to the maximum two-thirds pension at your normal retirement age, there is the possibility you may exceed it. And if you decide to stay on in a reduced capacity for a lower salary, your ultimate pension could end up being lower. This is not always the case as employers may base your pension on average earnings over an earlier period. So check first which definition of 'final salary' your employer uses when calculating your pension.

- **Money purchase schemes.** While you continue working, the value of your pension fund will continue to be boosted by further contributions and any investment growth. It will also buy a higher annuity when you eventually retire, because you will be older and therefore qualify for increased annuity rates. However, as with final salary schemes, there could be problems if you were already approaching the maximum two-thirds pension at your normal retirement age.

Personal pensions

There is considerable flexibility regarding the retirement date under a personal pension, although an annuity must be purchased by age 75 at the latest. There is no limit on the total benefits you can take from the pension so you can also go on contributing up to age 75, subject to the usual limits and the earnings cap. Alternatively, you can continue working and not make any further contributions. It is also possible to use part of your pension fund to provide a pension if you are working part-time and activate the remainder later when you stop working completely. (See Chapter 11 for more details of your retirement options under a personal pension plan.)

10 ‖ *Divorce and Death*

A pension can easily become one of your biggest investments, if not the biggest. This is especially the case for men who have contributed regularly to a pension for much of their working lives. For most women, on the other hand, the accumulation of a pension has tended to be more haphazard. Although the roles can be reversed, it is less usual. The main problem is that while a large percentage of women work nowadays, their career patterns often make it difficult for them to build up a substantial pension. They usually take career breaks to look after young children and may then only work part-time for some time thereafter. Until recently, company pension schemes did not always offer membership to part-timers. This means that many married women end up relying, to varying degrees, on their husbands' pension. So if a couple divorce, a pension becomes an important consideration. What happens to a pension on the death of a spouse or ex-spouse is also a matter of concern.

Couples who do not marry should look even more carefully at their pension arrangements. Women may find themselves severely disadvantaged in the event of a split although on death the situation is not quite so bleak if their partner was in the right sort of pension scheme.

Divorce

When a divorce occurs there are clear-cut procedures regarding the state pension scheme. The question of how best to deal with private pensions in a divorce settlement has been under discussion for many years and a proper solution to the problem has still not been reached.

The state pension

For younger women, a divorce is unlikely to have much effect on their state pension position. They will have been contributing to their own state pension and even if they have stopped working to look after children, they will qualify for Home Responsibilities Protection which will preserve their basic state pension rights.

Women who married before 1977, however, may have decided to pay the lower rate Married Woman's National Insurance contribution, which did not count towards a pension of their own. They will not lose out on their basic state pension rights, because their National Insurance record will be credited on the basis of their husbands' contributions, but they will not get any credit for SERPS benefits, even if their husbands were in the scheme.

After a divorce a woman will be responsible for her own contributions, so unless she still qualifies for Home Responsibilities Protection because she is looking after a child under 16 or a sick and disabled person at home, she will have to take a job or register as unemployed to continue her contribution record. However, if she is almost 60 and has been married for long enough, she may qualify for a full single person's basic state pension at 60 even if she pays no more contributions.

If a couple divorces after state pension age and one partner has a lower pension because of an insufficient contribution record, he or she can also benefit from the other partner's better record and move on to a higher pension. However, this will not include any SERPS pension which that partner may receive.

Private pensions

Until quite recently, pensions were often overlooked in divorce proceedings. After a divorce, an ex-wife could only claim part of her former husband's pension if there was a court order for maintenance. If her ex-husband remarried, any spouse's pension would be paid on his death to his current wife, although some trustees of employers' schemes do have the discretion to make payments to an ex-wife if she is still financially dependent on her former husband at the time of his death. Although it was possible for courts to award an ex-wife other assets in lieu of pension rights this was not often done.

In Scotland, pensions have been actively considered in divorces since the mid-1980s. The Family Law (Scotland) Act 1985 lays down that the values of the pension rights of each partner are to be included in the matrimonial property and those assets split equally. This covers all types of private pension arrangements, both occupational schemes and personal pension plans. The snag with this legislation is that it is not yet possible to divide up the pension benefits themselves, so it has meant that the value of other assets such as the family home was often given to the ex-wife in lieu of her share of the pension rights. There was no obligation for her to use the extra amounts she received to invest in a pension for herself.

The position in the rest of Britain is now covered by the Pensions Act 1995, which provides that a court can 'earmark' part of an occupational or personal pension for the benefit of a member's former or legally separated spouse. This means that when the member retires, a share of the retirement benefits becomes payable directly to the former partner. The provision applied to all divorce proceedings started from 1 July 1996 onwards and trustees of pension schemes and pension companies were required to start paying pensions to former spouses where required after 6 April 1997. The extra costs involved can be passed to the member.

When divorce proceedings start, pension scheme trustees and pension plan managers are obliged to co-operate. If requested by a member or his or her spouse, they must send details of a member's transfer value within three months. After a court has issued an order 'earmarking' part of someone's rights, if that person subsequently transfers these to another pension scheme, the trustees or managers of the former scheme must forward a copy of the court order to the new scheme within 14 days of the transfer being made. Within the same period they must also inform the member's former spouse when and where the transfer has been made. The earmarking order will continue to apply to the transferred rights in the new scheme unless the former spouse remarries and, as a result, the earmarking order ceases to be effective. The ex-spouse is expected to inform the pension scheme within 14 days of remarriage.

At retirement, the required part of the pension will be paid to the ex-spouse but when the member dies the pension stops too. There is no continuing ex-spouse's pension.

Future developments

Pensions earmarking has not solved the problem of how to achieve a fair division of pension benefits on divorce. A former spouse who is older than her ex-partner, for example, will not get any pension until he decides to take his pension, and she may experience financial hardship in the meantime. She will also lose the pension in the event of his death.

The alternative is 'pension splitting' or 'pension sharing' as the present Government prefers to describe it. This would enable the courts to order divorcing couples to divide up the pension at the time of the divorce settlement. It would allow a clean break to be made and each spouse would then be able to have a pension appropriate to his or her circumstances. The Government has recently announced it will introduce legislation to make this possible. Splitting would apply to SERPS as well as employers' and personal pensions. The legislation is expected to be implemented in 2000.

Death

When you have contributed to a pension for many years, it is comforting to know that your spouse will benefit from it after your death. However, there are still some anomalies in the treatment of widows and widowers.

The state pension

The treatment of widows and widowers under the state scheme depends partly on their ages at the date of death.

Widows
- **Widows under state pension age** receive a tax-free lump sum of £1,000 when their husbands die. A widowed mother's allowance is paid to a widow who has at least one child for whom she gets child benefit, or if she is expecting her late husband's baby.

  Widows who are aged 45 or over without eligible children when their husband dies, or when widowed mother's allowance ends, get a widow's pension. Between the ages of 45 and 55 this pension is on a sliding scale from 30% to the full single person's basic state pension.

  Women aged 55 are paid the full widow's pension immediately. In addition to the widowed mother's allowance and widow's pension, all women are also eligible for a SERPS pension based on their late husband's contribution record. If he dies before the year 2000, they can inherit his full SERPS pension; if he dies later they will receive 50% of it.

- **Widows over state pension age** receive a basic state retirement pension based on their husbands' contributions if they did not already receive a pension in their own right. They will also inherit his SERPS pension. Again, if he dies before the year 2000 they will get all of his additional pension, but if he dies later they will get 50%.

Widowers:
- **A widower whose wife dies before state pension age** receives no special state benefits even if he still has dependent children. (However, if his wife has opted out of SERPS and had that part of her NI contributions paid into an appropriate personal pension plan, he can receive a pension from the plan provided he is over 45 or has a child for whom he gets child benefit.) If

he has not remarried by state retirement age, he can have his own state pension based on his wife's contribution record if this produces a better pension for him.

- **A widower who is over state pension age when his wife dies** can have his pension boosted if his wife's contribution record was better than his and he can also inherit her SERPS pension. However, both the basic and additional pension he receives cannot be any more than the maximum payable in each category to a single person at the time of her death. Moreover, even though his wife may have been contributing to SERPS since it started in 1978, he will only receive 50% of her entitlement since 1988, as this was when these widowers' pensions were first introduced.

Employers' pension schemes
Widows:
- **Before normal retirement age.** The widow of a pension scheme member who dies before retirement will normally receive a tax-free lump sum of three or four times her husband's salary at the time of his death. The provision of a spouse's pension and other benefits varies between schemes.

    In a final salary scheme, a spouse's pension is usually provided which is 50% of the member's accumulated pension rights plus some or all of the potential pension which the employee would have earned up to his normal pension age. In money purchase schemes, the approach is more varied. Many schemes pay out the value of the member's pension as a lump sum. A smaller proportion pay a spouse's pension only, while others pay both a return of fund and a spouse's pension.

    A pension may also be paid to the children of a member until they reach age 18 or cease full-time education. This is more usual in final salary than in money purchase schemes.

- **After retirement.** The maximum spouse's pension that can be paid by an employer's scheme is two-thirds of the employee's pension, but in final salary schemes it is more usual for it to be one-half. If a spouse is substantially younger than the scheme member, around three-quarters of private schemes will scale down the level of pension paid.

In most money purchase schemes, it is the member's own decision whether a spouse's pension is purchased at retirement, so it is possible that a spouse may get no pension at all.

Widowers: Nowadays employers are obliged to provide the same benefits for widowers of female members as they do for widows of male members both before and after retirement. However, most schemes did not introduce equality until 1988 or later and consequently many widowers' pensions are based only on their wives' service since that time even though they may have been members of a scheme for considerably longer.

Remarriage

Widows and widowers who receive a spouse's pension can lose it if they remarry. This is more likely to happen in the case of public sector schemes, but it can also apply with private company schemes. So widows and widowers should consider their position carefully as they are unlikely to be able to reclaim the pension if a subsequent marriage proves unsuccessful.

Personal pensions

If a personal pension has been used to contract out of the state earnings related pension scheme (SERPS), what happens to that part of the fund which has been built up from National Insurance rebates – the 'protected rights' element – when the policyholder dies will be different from what happens to that part built up from voluntary contributions. On death before retirement a spouse's pension will be payable from the protected rights element. Similarly at retirement, an annuity must be purchased which provides a 50% spouse's pension. What happens to the remaining fund varies according to whether death takes place before or after retirement.

- **Before retirement.** If a policyholder dies before taking any pension benefits, the full value of the pension fund will normally be paid to his or her estate as a lump sum. A spouse will be able to receive this money tax free, but if it passes to other beneficiaries there may be a liability to Inheritance Tax unless the policy has been written in trust. Another advantage of putting a policy in trust is that beneficiaries will not have to wait until probate has been granted.

  You should bear in mind that in the early years of your policy its value will be limited. So if you want to ensure your spouse or other dependants are better provided for, you should take out extra life insurance using part of your pension contribution allowance to claim tax relief on the premiums. This policy can also be written in trust.

  If you have an old-style retirement annuity policy, the amount paid out on death may be less than its full value so extra life insurance may be especially relevant. (See Chapter 5 for more details.)

- **After retirement.** Provision for a spouse will depend on the type of annuity that has been purchased at retirement. If the policyholder has bought an annuity for himself or herself only, then all pension payments might simply cease on death. However, even in these circumstances most people buy annuities which make payments for a guaranteed period of at least five years. If they die during that time the balance of the five years' income is paid into their estate.

  Couples can opt for a joint life annuity which will ensure that payments continue after the death of the purchaser. The remaining partner will have no access to the fund itself unless the policyholder has decided to defer the purchase of an annuity after retirement by means of an income drawdown arrangement or by taking a phased retirement. (See Chapter 11 for more details about personal pension retirement options.)

Unmarried Couples

Many couples now choose to live together without getting married. While this arrangement is becoming more and more socially acceptable, it can cause pension problems when a couple splits up or one partner dies.

If a couple part, it will not be possible to claim a state pension based on a partner's National Insurance record as you can after a divorce, although women with children will get Home Responsibilities Protection to cover their basic pension. No widow's pension will be provided if a partner dies. (The situation may be somewhat different in Scotland where co-habitation can be recognized as a form of marriage.)

A potentially much greater financial loss can arise when a couple split up from the fact that an unmarried partner will have no claim to a share in the other's private pension. When they first start living together, therefore, a partner with little or no pension provision of his or her own would be well advised to get the other to help build up a fund.

On the death of a member of a company scheme, an unmarried partner may be somewhat better off. Where life insurance is provided by a pension scheme before retirement, it is more common for members to be allowed to nominate whoever they want to receive that benefit which is normally a lump sum of between three and four times their annual salary.

What happens to your pension is another matter. According to the last annual survey by the National Association of Pension Funds, over two-thirds of private company schemes will provide a pension for an unmarried partner, but usually at the trustees' discretion. Before they do so, the trustees may look for some proof of a long-standing relationship and financial dependence on the deceased member, such as whether the couple had children or a joint mortgage.

Public sector pension schemes do not normally provide a pension for an unmarried partner, although they may pay benefits to a member's children even if the parents were unmarried. While a couple are both working this may not seem like a problem, but after retirement the surviving partner may face financial hardship if she does not inherit the pension.

With personal pensions, the position is somewhat more straightforward. If you die before retirement, your pension fund will be paid into your estate. Provided you have left a will setting out who should receive the money, then an unmarried partner can benefit. It is even better if the pension is written in trust so that there is no liability for inheritance tax. At retirement it is normally possible to buy a joint life annuity even if you are unmarried, and this will ensure that the surviving partner continues to receive a pension.

Same Sex Relationships

Couples in same sex relationships face an even more difficult situation. Although a growing number of pension scheme trustees are prepared to consider paying benefits to same sex partners, they still account for only around a third of private sector pension schemes and in the public sector the proportion is even lower. Also in most cases payments are dependent on the trustees' discretion.

With a personal pension, the pension fund will be paid into your estate if you die before retirement so this can be passed to whomever you choose. At retirement, it may be possible to buy a joint life annuity with a same sex partner. Another alternative would be to use the tax-free lump sum from your pension at retirement to buy an ordinary life annuity for your partner. (See Chapter 11 for more detail about annuities.)

11 ‖ *Retirement*

After years spent working and saving for your retirement, the time eventually comes when you can put your feet up and start drawing your pension. However, not everyone can relax straight away. There may be some crucial decisions that have to be made first, particularly if you have a personal pension or are thinking of transferring to a personal pension for extra flexibility. The type of annuity or income drawdown arrangement you choose in these circumstances will have a major impact on your future retirement income.

Most people will have at least one decision to make about whether or not to take part of their pension as a tax-free lump sum at retirement, although if you are a member of a public sector pension scheme you will normally get a lump sum automatically. The only pensions where there is no cash option are those which have been paid for by SERPS rebates alone.

Should You Take a Cash Sum?

How much tax free cash at retirement?

Employer's scheme	One and a half times final salary
Personal pension	25% of pension fund
Retirement annuity	Three times a single life annuity

Taking part of your pension as a cash lump sum at retirement will mean reducing the regular income you get from your pension. There are various advantages to taking cash – not least that it is tax free – but if you need as much retirement income as possible you will need to think the matter through carefully. For example, if you are a member of an employer's pension scheme which has a good record of providing discretionary increases to its pensioners, you may be better off in the long run taking a full pension. But if you have a personal pension, you might actually be able to increase your income by taking a lump sum. The reason is that while the income from a pension annuity is taxed as earned income, the income from a similar 'purchased life' annuity is taxed less harshly. So if you take the maximum tax-free cash and invest it in that type of annuity, you could end up with a higher net income.

Table 17: Personal pensions – extra pension versus extra annuity income

Man aged 65 with £40,000 pension fund	Full pension	Reduced pension +annuity income
Lump sum	–	£10,000
Pension fund	£40,000	£30,000
Pension annuity (net of 23% tax)	£2,888	£2,166
Purchased life annuity (net of 20% tax)	–	£846
Total net income	£2,888	£3,012

Source: Norwich Union

However, the disadvantage of taking all your pension as income is that you lose all future access to the capital. You may prefer to invest your tax-free cash in an income bond or a corporate bond PEP and accept a somewhat lower income, so that it remains available for you to spend or pass on to your children on your death. If you are in poor health, this is particularly relevant.

Other cash points:

- **AVCs.** Bear in mind that if you have made additional voluntary contributions to your pension through a scheme started before 8 April 1987, you can take all or part of their value in cash. The advantage of taking the AVCs as cash is that you must then give up less of your main company pension, which may qualify for pension increases. Any AVC or FSAVC arrangement started on or after 8 April 1987 can only be used to purchase an annuity.

- **Retirement annuities versus personal pensions.** If you still have an old-style retirement annuity plan taken out before 1988, the amount of tax-free cash you can take from your fund is not a fixed percentage as it is with a personal pension. The maximum is a sum equal to three times the pension produced by a single life annuity secured by the remaining value of the contract. Depending on your age and annuity rates at the time you retire, this calculation could produce a larger amount of tax-free cash than you might get from a personal pension. However, it would mean having to buy your annuity from the insurance company which issued your policy. You may be able to get a substantially better pension, and therefore be better off in the long run, by converting your policy to a personal pension so that you can shop around and get a more competitive annuity.

Other Decisions

Employers' pension schemes

- **Final salary schemes.** Apart from deciding whether to take tax-free cash or not, employees usually have no further decisions to make about their pension. The amount is predetermined according to their years of service and final salary, a spouse's pension is included automatically and future pension increases are laid down by law, with any additional increases decided by the employer and pension fund trustees.

  However, some people are now deciding to take transfer values from their pension funds at retirement and switch them into personal pensions so that they gain greater control and can utilize income drawdown schemes (see page 144 for details of how these schemes work). This route is only suitable for people with funds of at least £100,000 who are prepared to accept investment risk. It is vital to take independent financial advice if you are considering this option.

- **Money purchase schemes.** Members may have some choice in the type of pension annuity purchased when they reach retirement, depending on the rules of the scheme. For example, they may be able to decide whether or not an annuity which pays a spouse's pension should be purchased. However, for benefits acquired after April 1997, trustees are now required to buy annuities rising in line with inflation up to a maximum of 5% p.a. (limited price indexation).

  If you are given any say in the choice of annuities you should study all the options discussed below and also ensure that your trustees shop around for the best deal. For complete freedom of choice you could take a transfer value from your scheme at retirement and switch it into a personal pension instead. This would also enable you to take advantage of an income drawdown scheme. But if you do consider this course of action, it is essential to take independent financial advice.

Personal pensions

At some time between the ages of 50 and 75, holders of personal pensions must use their pension fund to buy an annuity to provide their retirement income. These annuities are contracts sold by insurance companies whereby, in exchange for a lump sum, they guarantee to provide you with a regular income until you die. So there is no danger of your money ever running out in your lifetime and payments can continue until the death of a partner, too.

A variety of factors determine how much pension you will get when you buy an annuity. The main influence is the level of long-term interest rates, but each company sets its own annuity rates and the variations can lead to significant differences in the amount of pension paid. Fortunately you are not restricted to buying an annuity from the company which has provided your pension plan. You are free to use what is called the 'open market option' and transfer your fund elsewhere to buy an annuity. This could increase your pension by 20% or more, depending on the type of annuity you choose, at no extra cost.

Another reason why it is important to shop around is that your pension company may not offer the full range of annuity options or types of annuity. Making the right decision is essential because once an annuity is purchased you cannot get your money back and no change in terms is possible.

Table 18: The importance of the open market option

Differences in the initial pensions available from two types of annuities, assuming a pension fund of £10,000.

Annuity Provider	Woman aged 60		Man aged 65		Man 65/Woman 60	
	Level Pension	Pension rising at 5% p.a.	Level Pension	Pension rising at 5% p.a.	Level Pension	Pension rising at 5% p.a.
Best rate	£803	£465	£979	£664	£813	£485
Worst rate	£736	£337	£923	£549	£762	£352
Difference	9%	38%	6%	21%	7%	38%

Annuities payable monthly in advance, without guarantee, pension from joint life annuity reduces by one-third on death of male.

Source: Moneyfacts, February 1998

Why Annuity Rates Vary

- **Age** is one of the key factors influencing the basic amount of pension you will get and is naturally one over which you have little control unless you are able to delay the purchase of your annuity (for ways of doing this see below under 'income draw-down' and 'phased retirement'). Your age is important because it determines the period over which the annuity companies anticipate having to spread their payments. They base their calculations on average life expectancies, so the older you are when you buy an annuity the more income you will get from a given size of pension fund. A 70-year-old, for example, would get a pension around 30% higher than a 60-year-old because of his or her shorter life expectancy.

- **Sex** also influences your life expectancy. Women are generally expected to live longer than men, so they will receive a lower pension than men of the same age. A 60-year-old woman, for example, would get a pension around 10% smaller than a man with the same fund to invest.

- **Health.** Standard annuity rates are calculated on the basis that you are in good health. However, if your health is very poor or there are other reasons why you might have a shorter life expectancy – for example, you are a regular smoker or you suffer from diabetes – some companies will give you a better pension. Medical evidence may be required.

- **Single or joint.** If you choose a single life annuity, your pension will normally cease immediately on your death. However, if you are married or live with someone as a couple you may prefer to opt for a joint life annuity. This way the pension will continue being paid to your spouse or partner after your death for the rest of his or her life. Same sex partners will be considered by some companies.

  The income paid to you under a joint life annuity will be less than you would get from a single life annuity. The reduction will depend on the age gap between you and your partner and how much pension will be paid after your death. A popular choice is 50%, but it can range between 33% and 100%. A partner's pension of 50% would typically reduce your starting pension by around 14%. This reduction will remain even if your partner dies before you.

- **Guarantee period.** Pension payments will normally cease on your death or that of the surviving partner in the case of a joint life annuity. However, you can build in a period of guaranteed payments, normally five or ten years. This means that full payments will continue even if you die during that period. A lump sum may be paid instead of income to cover the remainder of the guarantee period. The cost of a guarantee will vary according to your age and the length of the guarantee. The older you are and the longer the guarantee, the more it will reduce your pension. A 65-year-old would get around 3% less pension from an annuity with a five-year guarantee; with a ten-year guarantee the reduction would be about 8%.

If you have a joint life annuity, the full pension will normally be paid to the end of the guarantee period and the spouse's pension will continue thereafter.

- **Frequency of income.** You can choose whether you want your pension paid monthly, quarterly, half-yearly or yearly. Most people like the convenience of receiving it monthly. However, you could boost your income by around 7% if you had it paid annually.

Other options include a choice of having your pension paid either in advance or arrears. Advance payments start immediately your pension fund is handed over. But, not surprisingly, it is more beneficial to wait until the end of the period for payment. Although it only makes a slight difference if you are getting your pension monthly, it can boost your income by around 15% if you receive it annually in arrears instead of in advance.

If you do opt for annual payments, it would be wise to have your annuity paid 'with proportion', meaning that a proportionate amount would be paid if you died between payments. If you are taking a monthly pension, however, it is cheaper to settle for 'without proportion' payments. This way the last payment will be the one made before your death.

Types of Annuity

There are basically four main types of pension annuities:

Level annuities

As the name suggests, these annuities pay the same fixed amount every year throughout your retirement. Initially they provide the highest pension, which is why most people still choose them. The problem is that because the amount is fixed, its purchasing power will be gradually eroded by inflation. Fortunately, inflation is not as virulent nowadays as it was a few years ago. Nevertheless, even 3% inflation will have eaten away around a quarter of the value of your pension after ten years.

Escalating annuities
Payments made by these annuities increase each year at a predetermined rate of, say 3% or 5%. This can help to offset the effects of inflation in years to come. However the starting pension will be considerably lower than that provided by a level annuity. In the example below, the starting pension from a 3% p.a. escalating annuity would be around 22% less than a level pension.

The advantage is that an escalating pension will overtake the fixed pension after eight years. However, it would be 16 years before the

Table 19: Comparison of level and escalating annuities for a man of 65 based on a purchase price of £100,000

Year	Level annuity	Annuity escalating at 3% p.a.
	£ p.a.	£ p.a.
1	9,531	7,427
2	9,531	7,650
3	9,531	7,880
4	9,531	8,363
5	9,531	8,608
6	9,531	8,868
7	9,531	9,135
8	9,531	9,410
9	9,531	9,692
10	9,531	9,982
11	9,531	10,279
12	9,531	10,590
13	9,531	10,910
14	9,531	11,237
15	9,531	11,571
16	9,531	11,920
Total	152,496	153,522

total amount paid out by the escalating annuity exceeded the amount paid out from the level annuity – without taking inflation into account. Basically, the insurance company aims to pay you roughly the same amount over your expected lifespan with this type of annuity as it would with a level annuity. If you are in good health and your family tends to live longer than average, you could reap higher benefits from this type of annuity in the long term. If not, it may be better to opt for a level annuity and save some of your pension in the early years, if you can afford to, for later use.

Index-linked annuities

These annuities provide payments which are linked to the movements in the retail price index, giving absolute security that the value of your pension will not be eroded by inflation. Your pension will increase each year when inflation is rising, although in the event of negative inflation it would decrease. The main drawback of this type of annuity is that it too gives a lower starting pension than a level annuity, although as the outlook for inflation has improved the gap has narrowed. Nevertheless it is more difficult to predict when the total payments from this type of annuity will exceed the level version because of the uncertainty about future inflation.

Investment annuities

There are two main types of investment annuity – with profits and unit linked.

Under a with-profits annuity, your pension will consist of a basic element plus additional bonuses which will fluctuate in line with investment returns. It is possible for investors to draw part of the bonuses in advance and have them included in their annuity payments.

Traditionally, with-profits policies have produced returns in excess of inflation and a pension from this type of annuity could show a steady increase, but future bonuses are not guaranteed. If investment conditions are poor, there could be a cut in bonuses and your pension could go down in value.

With unit linked annuities, your fund buys units in an investment fund and the pension payments you receive will move in line with the bid value of these units, so they could go down as well as up. Over the long term, share related funds have produced better returns than the gilts and fixed interest securities in which ordinary annuities are invested. However, there is much more risk involved.

Table 20: Annuity choices

Initial gross pension available from different types of annuities bought with a fund of £100,000

	Man aged 65	Man aged 65/Woman aged 60*
	£ p.a.	£ p.a.
Level annuity	9,531	8,352
Annuity escalating at 3%	7,427	6,203
With-profits annuity	5,748	4,530
With-profits annuity assuming 3% bonus	7,651	6,399
Index linked annuity	7,322	6,097

* Pension payments payable monthly in advance, guaranteed five years, for joint life annuity pension reduces by half on death of male.

Source: Equitable Life

Which Annuity?

The first two categories of annuities listed above are the most popular because they offer guaranteed returns. They are also the most widely available. The rates they offer vary with long-term interest rates. They are mainly invested in Government securities and other fixed interest investments such as local authority loans. For this reason, it may be a good idea as you draw near retirement to switch your pension fund into investment funds which hold the same type of securities because their value will mirror annuity prices. Index-linked and investment annuities are offered by fewer companies. If you are interested in an investment linked annuity, it is important to check a company's investment performance.

When you are choosing an annuity you will need to ask yourself the following questions:

- **How much income do I need?** Many people need as much income as they can get from their pension fund because they have not saved enough in the past, so they have to choose a level annuity. However, in the long run you may get more from an annuity which increases over time.
- **How will my spouse/partner manage when I die?** Unless your spouse has an adequate pension in his or her own right, you should arrange a joint life annuity.
- **How long am I going to live?** An impossible question to answer, but if both your parents have lived to a ripe old age, the chances are you may too, so you need an annuity that will provide for you over the long term.
- **How much risk can I cope with?** If stock market fluctuations mean you would be unable to sleep at night, a unit linked annuity won't be for you. However, if you have a good basic pension from a company and are wondering what type of annuity to buy with your AVCs then you may be prepared to take more risk.

Once you have bought an annuity it is impossible to reverse your decision, but fortunately it does not have to be an either/or choice. It may be a good idea to split your pension fund and use, say, half to buy a level annuity and half for a with profits annuity.

To find out which companies are currently paying the best annuity rates for straightforward level or increasing annuities, you could look in the weekend press or use the Moneyfacts fax service. But bear in mind that published tables are based on specific ages. Companies which are competitive for one age may not have such good rates as another, so ask for your own quotes from a shortlist of companies and make sure they are on the same basis. Or better still, contact a specialist annuity adviser for help in shopping round. If you are interested in a with-profits annuity or you have health problems, it is not advisable to try to do it yourself.

Delaying Your Annuity Purchase

Nowadays there are ways of delaying the purchase of annuities at retirement while still taking some income from your pension fund in the meantime. This approach can be particularly useful for people who have other resources or are going into semi-retirement only and require just a modest income from their pension fund. However, these schemes are only advisable for people with substantial pension funds (at least £100,000 but ideally £200,000 or more) or who have other sources of retirement income. Otherwise the costs and the risks are likely to be too high.

There are a number of possible advantages in delaying your annuity purchase. Your pension fund will remain invested in shares and other assets which could produce better returns than that achieved by buying an annuity, which is basically a fixed interest investment. Interest rates may go up, so that annuity rates will be higher in future. Part of your fund will remain available to pass on to your family should you die before 75 (the latest age at which an annuity must be purchased). When you do buy you will be older, so annuity rates will be higher because your life expectancy will be reduced.

However, there are a number of potential disadvantages, too. In order to achieve the investment returns necessary to outperform an ordinary annuity, you will need to leave your fund substantially invested in shares with can fluctuate in value. If the investment performance of your fund is poor its value may go down, leaving you worse off than if you had bought an annuity. Interest rates may fall instead of rising, bringing annuity rates down in the future. What's more, although it may be beneficial to put off an annuity purchase if you are still in your fifties to take advantage of higher annuity rates when you are older, you must also consider the annuity income you are losing for each year that you defer your investment. Once you get to 65 you could be losing more income than you will eventually gain from higher annuity rates.

There are two ways in which you can put off your annuity purchase. One arrangement is known as 'income drawdown' and the other is called 'phased retirement'. In both cases it is vital to take expert advice from a specialist independent financial adviser.

Income Drawdown

Which plan?
The first step is to consider your choice of provider. Although income drawdown is a relatively new concept, an increasing number of personal pension companies now offer this facility as an option to existing investors. However, there is no need to remain with the same company that you have saved with.

Many advisers recommend transferring to a 'self-invested personal pension' (SIPP) – if you do not already have one – before starting your income drawdown plan. These plans give you freedom of investment in a wide range of assets including shares, gilts, unit and investment trusts, insurance funds, futures and options, commercial property and deposit accounts.

The main advantage is that you will not be stuck with one set of investment managers which could be a disaster if they do not perform well, as you are not permitted to move your fund once you have you have started an income drawdown plan. SIPP providers include insurance companies, stockbrokers and other professional advisers.

You must consider your investment strategy carefully. You will have to be prepared to invest all or most of your fund in shares in order to have a good chance of achieving a return that will match the income you would have received by investing in an annuity immediately. In fact, you will need a somewhat better return if you are going to cover the cost of the SIPP. If you do not want to do the job of managing the fund yourself, many providers will do it on your behalf through a discretionary management service.

Regular reviews of your fund performance will have to be carried out. Your financial adviser should do one every year and the product provider is also legally obliged to conduct a review every three years.

If a fund has performed badly, you may be advised to buy an annuity immediately. No further contributions can be made to a pension plan once it has been converted to an income drawdown plan, though if you have eligible income you could set up another ordinary personal pension plan.

Cash and income

You will have to decide at the outset whether you want to take the tax-free cash from your income drawdown plan. If you don't take it then, the option will lapse and you will no longer be able to take out any cash even when you buy your annuity.

Once you have set your income drawdown plan in motion by taking a cash sum you will also have to start drawing an income. The minimum and maximum amount you can take is laid down by the Government Actuary's department. Basically, the maximum income you can draw is in line with the income which would be provided by a standard single life level annuity, the minimum is 35% of that figure. The amounts will be the same for every income drawdown plan. As long as you stay within these limits, you can change the level of income you take from the plan.

The income is subject to tax. It is paid net of basic rate tax and higher rate taxpayers will be assessed for further tax when they complete their tax return.

You will have to use your fund to buy an annuity by the time you reach your 75th birthday.

What happens on death

If you die before age 75, your remaining pension fund can be used in one of the four following ways:

- Your spouse can continue to take an income but must buy an annuity by his or her 75th birthday or the date you would have reached that age, whichever is earlier.
- Your spouse can buy an annuity immediately.
- Your spouse can take the fund as a lump sum, less 35% tax.

- If you were not married, the money will be returned to your
  estate, also less 35% tax. Unless you have written the death
  benefits in trust, it may also be liable to inheritance tax.

Phased Retirement

Phased retirement is a way of gradually converting your fund into
annuities and building up your regular pension. This type of arrangement can be particularly useful if you are self-employed and want to
reduce your workload in stages. All you need for such a scheme is a
fund which is divided between a number of policies. Nowadays it is
usual for companies to issue their pension policies in a number of
'segments'. This means you can take the benefits you need from a
limited number of segments each year leaving the remainder invested.

Table 21: Phased retirement – the principle

	Year 1	Year 2	Year 3	Year 4	Year 5
Pension fund					
Available fund	£200,000	£180,000	£160,000	£140,000	£120,000
Fund encashed	£20,000	£20,000	£20,000	£20,000	£20,000
Remaining fund	£180,000	£160,000	£140,000	£120,000	£100,000
Income					
Tax free cash	£5,000	£5,000	£5,000	£5,000	£5,000
Income from annuity	£1,500	£1,500	£1,500	£1,500	£1,500
Add income from existing annuities	£0	£1,500	£3,000	£4,500	£6,000
Total gross income	£6,500	£8,000	£9,500	£11,000	£12,500
Less income tax on annuities of 23%	£345	£690	£1,035	£1,380	£1,725
Total net income	£6,155	£7,310	£8,465	£9,620	£10,775

The table is purely for illustration and assumes that annuity rates do not
change and there is no investment growth in the remaining pension fund.

Source: The Annuity Bureau

Under this system, it is the combination of the tax-free cash you get from these segments plus the payments from the annuity bought with the balance which make up your total income. The income from the annuities alone in the first few years will be relatively modest, which is why it has to be supplemented with the tax-free cash. But as each year goes by the income from all the annuities will mount up steadily to provide a full pension eventually.

The advantage of this approach, as with income drawdown, is that part of your pension fund can remain invested in a spread of real assets, such as shares, and can continue to grow in a favourably taxed environment. By spreading your annuity purchases over a number of years, you will also be hedging your bets as far as interest rates are concerned rather than locking into the rates prevailing at one particular point in time.

However, as with income drawdown, there is the risk that investment conditions may become unfavourable and your remaining fund may fall instead of rising in value. Also, there is the disadvantage that you cannot take your tax-free cash in one big lump sum, so it may not be an option if you need the cash to repay a mortgage or you want to use it for something like the holiday of a lifetime. Some people get round this problem by using a combination of phased retirement with income drawdown.

12 | *Pension Problems*

In recent years the financial regulation of pensions has become increasingly tough, chiefly in reaction to some awful scandals. In the case of employers' schemes, it was the Robert Maxwell scandal which prompted the introduction of the 1995 Pensions Act. On the personal pensions side, companies and advisers have been subject to progressively tighter controls since the mis-selling of personal pensions came to light in the early 1990s. There are also a variety of safety nets in place. The Pensions Compensation Board will recompense members of company schemes whose employers take money dishonestly from the pension fund and become bankrupt. The Policyholders Protection Act, covering investors in pension policies or annuities issued by insurance companies, guarantees policyholders 90% of any money due if an insurance company fails. The Investor's Compensation Scheme will pay out to clients of financial advisers who have acted improperly.

However, many other types of individual pensions problems can arise. Naturally, it makes sense to try and avoid them in the first place by clarifying your position properly before you enter into any pension arrangement. When it is an employer's scheme, you will generally have to rely on the trustees and/or your employer to ensure that everything runs smoothly. If you seek individual advice about your pension, be sure you know exactly what type of adviser you are dealing with.

The main types of financial advisers are:

- **Company representatives.** If you ask a company representative about pensions, you will only be recommended the products offered by his or her company. Some companies employ hundreds of sales staff to visit people in their homes or places of work to sell their products. They are usually paid a basic salary plus commission or commission only. Recently it has become popular for companies to set up telephone selling operations for consumers who prefer to deal direct with their sales staff. It is not necessarily a bad thing to deal with company representatives, but it will be up to you to find out how that company's products compare with others.

- **Appointed representatives.** Like company representatives, appointed representatives can recommend the pension products of only one company but they may also engage in other types of business. For example, many building societies besides providing mortgages and savings accounts also sell the life and pension policies of certain insurance companies. In recent years, societies have derived considerable extra income from the commission they get from the sales of these products. You won't know whether the pension they are offering you is the best deal for you unless you make your own comparisons.

- **Independent financial advisers.** These advisers must look at the whole range of pension products available in the market and recommend the policy which they believe will meet your needs best. They vary from one-man operations to large nationwide firms. Some concentrate on selling pensions, insurance and investment products. Others are part of larger organizations. Many banks can provide independent financial advice if requested. If you require the name of an independent financial adviser who gives pensions advice you can contact IFA Promotion (see Appendix II for the address) which will provide you with the names of three companies located near to where you live or work. To cover the cost of the advice they give, advisers will normally take a commission from the company whose pension they have sold. However if you would prefer to pay a fee, there are a growing number of fee-based advisers. You can obtain a list of several in your area from the Money Management Register of Fee Based Advisers (See Appendix II).

- **Other professionals.** Independent financial advice is also provided by many accountants, actuaries and solicitors. They can give specialist advice on various aspects of your pension: an actuary could evaluate your transfer value from a company pension scheme, for example, and a pensions lawyer could advise you on legal aspects. Their advice will have to be paid for.

Where to Complain

If a problem does arise with your pension, there are various complaints procedures. Always remember when making a complaint to put it in writing and keep a copy of the correspondence. Send copies of policy documents and benefit statements to back up your claim, not the originals. The main complaints procedures are:

State pensions

It is not only individuals who can find the complexity of state pension arrangements leaves them confused about how much pension they can expect. It can also lead to mistakes being made by the Department of Social Security. If you believe an error has been made in the calculation of your pension, you can request a review or make an appeal. DSS leaflet NI 260 'A Guide to Reviews and Appeals' explains how the procedures work.

The first step is to ask for a full explanation of how your pension was calculated from your local DSS office. If you are not satisfied, you can ask the office which made the first decision to review your case. If the adjudication officer does not change the decision, you can then appeal to the social security appeal tribunal. You will normally have three months to appeal. The form in leaflet NI 246 'How to appeal', available from DSS offices, can be used. Keep a copy of the form and any other documents you send. When the hearing takes place you will have an opportunity to put your case.

Personal pensions

If you have a complaint about a personal pension, you can contact the Personal Investment Authority Ombudsman. The PIA is the main body which regulates firms that sell investments, including pensions, to the public.

However, in the first place you must write to the pension company or advisers concerned and ask them to investigate your problem. Address your letter to the 'Compliance Officer' at the head office of the firm and head it 'Complaint'. Member firms of the PIA are expected to acknowledge your complaint within seven business days and complete the investigation of the complaint within two months of receiving it.

If you are not satisfied with the outcome of the firm's investigation of your complaint, or it has not completed its investigation within two months, you can take your complaint to the PIA Ombudsman. You should send your complaint to the Ombudsman within six months of receiving a reply from the firm telling you of the outcome of its deliberations.

The Ombudsman will look into your case and if he finds your complaint justified he may then make a financial award against the firm of up to £100,000. The ruling is binding on the company, although you are free to pursue your case through the courts if you remain dissatisfied. The Ombudsman will not deal with complaints about falls in the value of a pension caused by market movements or with the basis of calculation of transfer values, maturity values or bonus rates.

Employers' pension schemes

Every pension scheme must have a clear complaints procedure for scheme members who have a complaint about their own pension. These complaints procedures are often called the 'internal dispute resolution procedures'. There are two stages. First, a named person who is responsible for dealing with complaints will look into your problem and try to resolve it. If you are not satisfied after that, you can ask the pension scheme's trustees to look into your complaint.

If you are still not happy, you can turn to the Occupational Pensions Advisory Service, which has experienced advisers throughout the

United Kingdom. You can contact your local adviser through your nearest Citizens' Advice Bureau or through OPAS central office (see Appendix II for the address).

OPAS may be able to deal with the complaint itself by confirming that a scheme has acted correctly and explaining the reason why. Otherwise it may suggest how you could approach the scheme again or it may deal with the scheme on your behalf to sort out the matter. Although it can negotiate with a scheme, it does not have enforcement powers.

If OPAS is unable to achieve a solution, and believes your complaint is justified, it will pass it on to the Pensions Ombudsman who has statutory powers to enforce his decisions. If the Ombudsman investigates and decides in your favour, he can award compensation if appropriate. His decision is binding on you and the pension scheme, although both parties can appeal to the High Court on a point of law.

APPENDIX I || *Glossary – Pension Terms Explained*

Accrual rate. The amount by which a pension builds up in an employer's pension scheme. This is usually a fraction like one-sixtieth or one-eightieth of an employee's earnings for each year of membership of the scheme.

Added years. Employers' pension schemes often calculate a final pension on the basis of how many years a member has belonged to the scheme. Some schemes allow members to buy additional years of membership with extra contributions. The advantage is that the extra pension is a guaranteed percentage of salary at retirement.

Additional voluntary contributions. Extra savings that can be made by members of employers' pension schemes to increase their pensions. The investments are usually managed by another organization, such as a building society or insurance company. Total contributions to the main scheme plus AVC contributions can amount to a maximum 15% of pay. The amount of extra pension is not guaranteed.

Allocation rate. The amount of each pension premium which is invested after some charges have been deducted. Typically it is around 95–100%, but it may be substantially less in the early years of a regular savings plan. High allocations may be offset by higher charges.

Annuity. A guaranteed income for life paid out in return for a lump sum. The amount of income depends on interest rates and a person's age and sex.

Appropriate personal pension. A pension plan into which National

Insurance rebates have been paid for an employee who has contracted out of the state earnings related pension scheme (SERPS). A pension cannot be taken from these plans until normal state retirement age, and no part can be taken as cash.

Band earnings. The amount of earnings between a lower and upper limit on which employees pay National Insurance contributions. The amount is adjusted each year. For 1998/99 the lower earnings limit is £3,328 and the upper limit is £25,220. It is also the amount on which a person's SERPS entitlement is based.

Benefit statement. A regular statement provided for employees in a company pension scheme showing the estimated amount of pension they can expect.

Bid/offer spread. When pension contributions are invested, this is the difference between the price at which units are bought in an investment fund – the offer price – and their value when redeemed – the bid price. The spread, typically 5%, creates an initial charge every time you invest.

Buyout bond. One of the investment choices for those who take a transfer value from their old employer's pension scheme. Offered by insurance companies, these bonds can provide better death benefits pre-retirement than a personal pension. Larger tax-free lump sums may also be available than through a personal pension.

Capital units. Investment units purchased in the early years of some pension plans which bear a higher annual management charge than ordinary units.

Carry back. A provision which allows personal pension contributions paid in one tax year to be treated for tax purposes as though they have been paid the year before.

Carry forward. A provision which allows personal holders to top up on contributions that were below the maximum permitted level over the previous six years.

Commutation. Taking part of a pension fund as a tax-free lump sum.

Compulsory purchase annuity. An annuity bought at retirement with a pension fund accumulated in a money purchase pension arrangement.

Contracted out. The facility to opt out of the state earnings related pension scheme and have a private pension instead. Individuals who opt out have a rebate of part of their National Insurance contributions paid into an appropriate personal pension. Most employers' pension schemes are contracted out. They pay reduced NI contributions and invest the difference in their pension scheme. Some smaller schemes are contracted in, i.e. employees are still members of SERPS but they can contract out on an individual basis if they wish to do so.

Contribution limits. Inland Revenue limits on how much can be paid into a pension. In an employer's scheme, employees can pay up to 15% of earnings. In a personal pension, the limit is between 17.5% and 40% depending on age.

Contributions. Payments made into a pension scheme.

Death benefits. Cash or pension paid to a deceased person's estate or dependants.

Deferred benefit. The pension which is held for an ex-member of an employer's scheme until he or she reaches retirement.

Defined benefit scheme. See final salary scheme.

Defined contribution scheme. See money purchase scheme.

Discretionary benefits. In an employer's pension scheme, these are typically increases in pensions or payments to partners other than a member's spouse which are not guaranteed under the scheme rules. They are paid at the discretion of the scheme's trustees.

Earnings cap. The maximum amount of salary on which pension contributions and benefits can be based. Introduced in 1989, it applies to personal pensions and to members of employer's schemes set up after March 1989 or members who joined a scheme after 1 June 1989.

Executive pension scheme. A money purchase pension scheme set up for individual directors or executives which has the same limits as an employer's scheme.

Final salary scheme. Employers' pension schemes in which the pension is a guaranteed fraction of an employee's salary at or around retirement, normally either 1/60th or 1/80th, for each year of service.

Funded unapproved retirement benefit (furb). Pension schemes set up by employers to provide extra benefits for employees affected by the earnings cap. They are not approved for tax purposes, so employers' contributions are taxed as a benefit in kind and the fund is subject to tax. However, the total benefit can be taken as a tax-free lump sum at retirement.

Graduated pension. An additional state pension to which employees contributed between April 1961 and April 1965.

Group personal pension. A series of individual personal pension policies arranged for employees by an employer. Joint contributions are normally made by the employer and employee, but the employer has no legal rights over the scheme. The employee is the owner of the policy.

Guaranteed minimum pension. Until April 1997, the pension provided by final salary pension schemes as a replacement for SERPS had to be at least as big as SERPS. Now these schemes have been put on a par with money purchase schemes and personal pensions where there is no such guarantee.

Illustration. A projection showing what your pension may be worth at retirement, after deduction of charges and assuming growth rates laid down by the Personal Investment Authority. All pension providers must use the same rates of growth. The figures are not guaranteed.

Income drawdown or withdrawal. An arrangement which allows those with personal pensions to defer buying an annuity but to draw an income from their fund in the meantime. Only advisable for large funds of £100,000-plus and for investors prepared to accept risk.

Independent financial adviser. Authorized intermediaries who are not tied to one company and can advise on and deal with products from all companies on the market. They are normally paid by commission from the companies whose products they sell. Some charge a fee.

Independent trustee. A person or professional firm appointed by the insolvency practitioner to run the pension schemes of companies which go bust.

Integration. Integrated company pension schemes pay a reduced pension to take account of the fact that employees will receive a basic state pension; contributions are accordingly lower.

Investment fund. Pool of money formed from policy holders' pension premiums which is invested in one or more types of assets, such as shares, property, and fixed-interest securities.

Key features document. Part of the paperwork sent to you before you take out a pension giving brief details of the plan and an illustration showing the charges which will be deducted and what your pension may be worth at retirement assuming standard growth rates.

Last survivor annuity. An annuity for two people where payments continue until the last person has died.

Limited price indexation (LPI). The minimum level at which post-1997 occupational and appropriate personal pensions must increase when in payment. They must rise by the lesser of the retail prices index or 5% per annum.

Lower earnings limit. The level of pay at which employees start paying National Insurance contributions.

Money purchase scheme. A pension scheme where contributions are invested in a fund which is normally used to buy an annuity at retirement. The amount of pension is not guaranteed.

National Insurance rebate. That part of a person's National Insurance contributions which is paid by the Department of Social Security into an appropriate personal pension if he or she chooses to opt out of the state earnings related pension scheme (SERPS).

Occupational pension scheme. A scheme to provide pensions for employees organized by an employer.

Open market option. The option to transfer the proceeds of your pension at retirement to another annuity provider.

Paid up pension policy. The name given to a regular premium pension policy in which past savings remain invested but to which no new premiums are added.

Pension mortgage. An arrangement under which it is agreed that the lump sum from your pension scheme at retirement will be used to pay off your mortgage.

Pensionable pay. The earnings on which an employee's pension and contributions to an employer's pension scheme are calculated. They may or may not include bonuses or overtime.

Personal pensions. Individual pension plans introduced in July 1988 which allow employees who are not members of employers' pension schemes or are self-employed to make their own pension provision.

Phased retirement. A process, also known as staggered vesting, where a pension fund is used to buy annuities over several years, leaving the balance of the fund invested.

Protected rights. The fund which contains the rebates of National Insurance contributions under a personal pension and other types of money purchase pensions. The fund cannot be used to buy a pension until state retirement age and the annuity purchased must be a joint life one which rises in line with the retail price index to a maximum of 5% p.a.

Reduction in yield. A figure found in key features documents which shows by how much the charges on a personal pension fund will reduce a given rate of investment growth. It is a useful means of making comparisons with other plans.

Retirement annuity contract. A type of personal pension issued before June 1988, sometimes referred to as a Section 226 policy. It has different contribution limits and the amount of tax-free cash is calculated differently, but it can be converted to a personal pension at any time.

Salary sacrifice. An arrangement where an employee forgoes part of his pay so that this can be paid directly into his pension by his employer. No National Insurance contributions are payable on these contributions.

Self invested personal pension (SIPP). A personal pension where funds can be spread among a range of investments including shares, gilts and unit trusts. You are not restricted to one investment manager. It is only suitable for large funds.

Small self-administered scheme (SSAS). A company pension scheme for small businesses which allows a degree of self-investment.

State earnings related pension scheme (SERPS). Set up in 1978 to provide employees with an additional pension to the basic retirement pension. The pension is linked to their earnings between the upper and lower earnings limits for National Insurance contributions. Employees may be contracted out of SERPS through a company pension scheme. Since 1988, individuals have also been able to opt out into their own personal pension.

Transfer value. The cash value of the pension you have built up in one scheme that can be transferred to another. In a final salary employer's scheme, it is calculated by an actuary to take into account the likely value of your pension rights when you retire. In a money purchase arrangement or personal pension, it is the value of your fund less any penalties.

Trustees. People appointed to run a pension scheme in accordance with the rules set down in the trust deed and in the best interests of the members. Trustees may include representatives of management and scheme members.

Unit linked pension fund. An investment fund divided up into units of equal worth. Units are allocated to your pension each time you make a contribution. The value, i.e. the price, of the units directly depends on the value of the underlying assets which can go down as well as up.

Upper earnings limit. No National Insurance contributions are paid on earnings above this limit, which is revised annually.

Waiver of premium. An option under a regular premium pension policy under which you pay a small charge in return for the pension company maintaining your contributions should you become too ill to work.

With profits fund. An investment fund which holds a mixture of assets. Pension holders receive a share of the profits from the fund in the form of annual and final bonuses. In determining annual bonuses, which are guaranteed once declared, a company's actuaries aim to smooth out investment fluctuations. The final bonus can be more volatile, depending on investment conditions, and is not guaranteed.

Written in trust. Writing a pension on life insurance policy in trust allows the proceeds to pass to beneficiaries free of inheritance tax on death. Most modern day pension plans are automatically written in trust. Older policies may need to be put in trust. Pension providers can supply the necessary forms.

APPENDIX II ‖ *Useful Names and Addresses*

Annuity Advisers

The Annuity Bureau,
Enterprise House,
59–65 Upper Ground,
London SE1 9PQ
Tel 0171 620 4090

Annuity Direct,
32 Scrutton Street,
London EC2A 4SS
Tel 0171 684 5000

Department of Social Security

All Social Security leaflets are available free of charge from your
local Social Security Office: see under Benefits Agency in the business
numbers section of your phone book, or Contributions Agency for
National Insurance.

If you are abroad and have an enquiry about UK NI contributions
or require a retirement pension forecast, contact the Contributions
Agency International Services, Longbenton, Newcastle upon Tyne
NE98 1YX, Tel 06451 54811. If you have an enquiry about benefits,
contact the Benefits Agency Pensions and Overseas Benefits Director-
ate, Department of Social Security, Tyneview Park, Whitley Road,
Benton, Newcastle upon Tyne, NE98 1BA, Tel 0191 218 7777.

Independent Financial Advisers

For the names of three independent financial advisers in your area, you can ring the IFAP Hotline on 0171 971 1177.

For the names of several fee-based independent financial advisers, ring 0117 976 9444, or write to The Money Management Register of Fee Based Advisers, Matrix Data Ltd, Freepost 22 (SW1465), London W1E 7EZ.

Ombudsmen

Pensions Ombudsman,
11 Belgrave Road,
London SW1V 1RB
Tel 0171 834 9144

Personal Investment Authority Ombudsman Bureau,
Hertsmere House,
Hertsmere Road,
London E14 4AB
0171 216 0016

Pensions Organizations

National Association of Pension Funds (NAPF),
12–18 Grosvenor Gardens,
London SW1W 0DH
Tel 0171 730 0585

Occupational Pensions Advisory Service (OPAS),
11 Belgrave Road,
London SW1V 1RB
Tel 0171 233 8080

Pension Schemes Registry,
PO Box 1NN,
Newcastle upon Tyne NE00 1NN
Tel 0191 225 6394

Pre-Retirement Courses

Pre-Retirement Association,
9 Chesham Road,
Guildford,
Surrey GU1 3LS
Tel 01483 301170

Professional Organizations

The Association of Consulting Actuaries,
1 Wardrobe Place,
London EC4V 5AH
Tel 0171 236 5514

Society of Pension Consultants,
Bartholomew House,
92 Fleet Street,
London EC4A 2AB
Tel 0171 353 1688

Publications

Money Management,
Third Floor,
Maple House,
149 Tottenham Court Road,
London W1P 9LL
Tel 0171 896 2525

Planned Savings,
33 Bowling Green Lane,
London EC1R 0DA
Tel 0171 837 1685

Moneyfacts,
66–70 Thorpe Road,
Norwich NR1 1BJ
Tel 01603 476747

INDEX